Basic Construction Blueprint Reading

Second Edition

Mark W. Huth

 DELMAR PUBLISHERS INC.®

NOTICE TO THE READER

Delmar Staff

Associate Editor: Marjorie A. Bruce
Editing Manager: Barbara A. Christie
Project Editor: Ruth East

Design Coordinator: Susan Mathews
Publications Coordinator: Karen Seebald

For information, address Delmar Publishers Inc.
3 Columbia Circle, PO Box 15015
Albany, New York 12212-5015

Printed in the United States of America
Published simultaneously in Canada
by Nelson Canada,
A division of The Thomson Corporation

Library of Congress Cataloging-in-Publication Data

Huth, Mark W.
    Basic construction blueprint reading.

    Includes index.
    1. Building--Details--Drawings. 2. Blueprints.
I. Title.
TH2031.H76 1989   692'.1   88-28505
ISBN O-8273-3233-5 (pbk.)
ISBN O-8273-3234-3 (instructor's guide)

Contents

Section 2 Math for Construction

Section 3 Trade Sketching

Section 4 Elements of Light Construction

Unit

Section 5 Reading Construction Drawings

Unit

Preface

Basic Construction Blueprint Reading, 2nd edition is a textbook for anyone who needs to learn how to understand the drawings used in the construction industry. Although the blueprint process is no longer used to make construction prints, it has become common practice to refer to all prints as blueprints. People who work in the building trades, building materials sales, real estate, construction estimating, and construction management all need to understand construction drawings. Print reading skills improve as they are used, so this book provides frequent opportunities to use the skills as they are learned.

To understand and use the information on construction prints requires the use of some very basic mathematics. Therefore, this edition includes a section on math. This section is as brief as possible, giving only the steps of the mathematical operations and examples. Even in situations where math is not the subject to be learned, this brief treatment will help you review where necessary.

Drawings and the prints made from drawings are the tools of communication for the construction industry. The need to use this form of communication is not limited to drafters, so this book includes a short section on sketching.

Each of the units in this textbook is designed to make learning easy. The units are short, and the content of the unit can easily be completed in a single lesson. The objectives at the beginning of the unit tell you and your instructor what to expect from the unit. At the end of each unit there are several assignment questions that require you to use what you should have learned by studying the unit. Most of the print reading units include questions that require you to read the prints for a small home. These are the prints at the back of the book. The sketching units have sketching assignments.

There is an instructor's guide available for *Basic Construction Blueprint Reading* 2nd edition. The instructor's guide includes answers to the textbook assignment questions, a bank of additional test questions, and masters from which the instructor can make overhead transparencies, worksheets, and other instructional aides.

ACKNOWLEDGMENTS

The instructor's listed below provided recommendations for the second edition of the text. The author expresses his appreciation to them for highlighting areas to be improved.

Ron Howard, Springfield-Clark County Joint Vocational-Technical School, Springfield, OH

Rodney Gray, Southern Maine Vocational-Technical Institute, S. Portland, ME

Deborah Christofferson, Onandaga, Cortland, Madison BOCES, Syracuse, NY

Richard Simmons, Daytona Beach Community College, Daytona Beach, FL

Curtis Corley, Randolph County Vocational-Technical Center, Elkins, WV

The following instructors provided detailed reviews of the revised text. Their comments and suggestions for improvements provided valuable guidance to the author.

James Northrup, Gates Chili Central School, Rochester, NY

Juan Serret, Bullard-Havens Regional Vocational-Technical School,
Bridgeport, CT

Section 1
Basic Blueprint Reading

UNIT 1   Introduction to Construction Drawings

OBJECTIVES

After completing this unit, you will be able to:

- explain the importance of drawings in construction.
- describe the diazo method of reproducing drawings.
- describe what is meant by computer-aided drafting.

THE IMPORTANCE OF DRAWINGS

The construction of a building involves many people working at different locations. Architects and engineers design the project, bankers and the owner finance the job, and building trades workers construct it. Each of these groups needs to communicate with the others. Construction drawings are used for this communication.

As the design professionals — the architects and engineers — develop their design, they make rough notes and sketches. Drafters prepare working drawings from these notes and sketches. These working drawings give information about the size, shape, and location of all parts of the structure to others involved with the project, figure 1-1.

In order to insure that these drawings will be interpreted the same by everyone who reads them, rigid rules are followed. Such things as the weight of lines, the location of dimensions, and the position of the views can affect the meaning of a drawing. To read and understand construction drawings accurately, it is important to understand these rules.

DIAZO PROCESS

When the drafter in the architect's or engineer's office completes a set of working drawings, copies must be made to give to all necessary personnel. The original working drawings are stored in the architect's or engineer's office for future reference. Making these copies is called *reproduction.*

The most widely used method of reproduction uses ammonia vapor as a developing

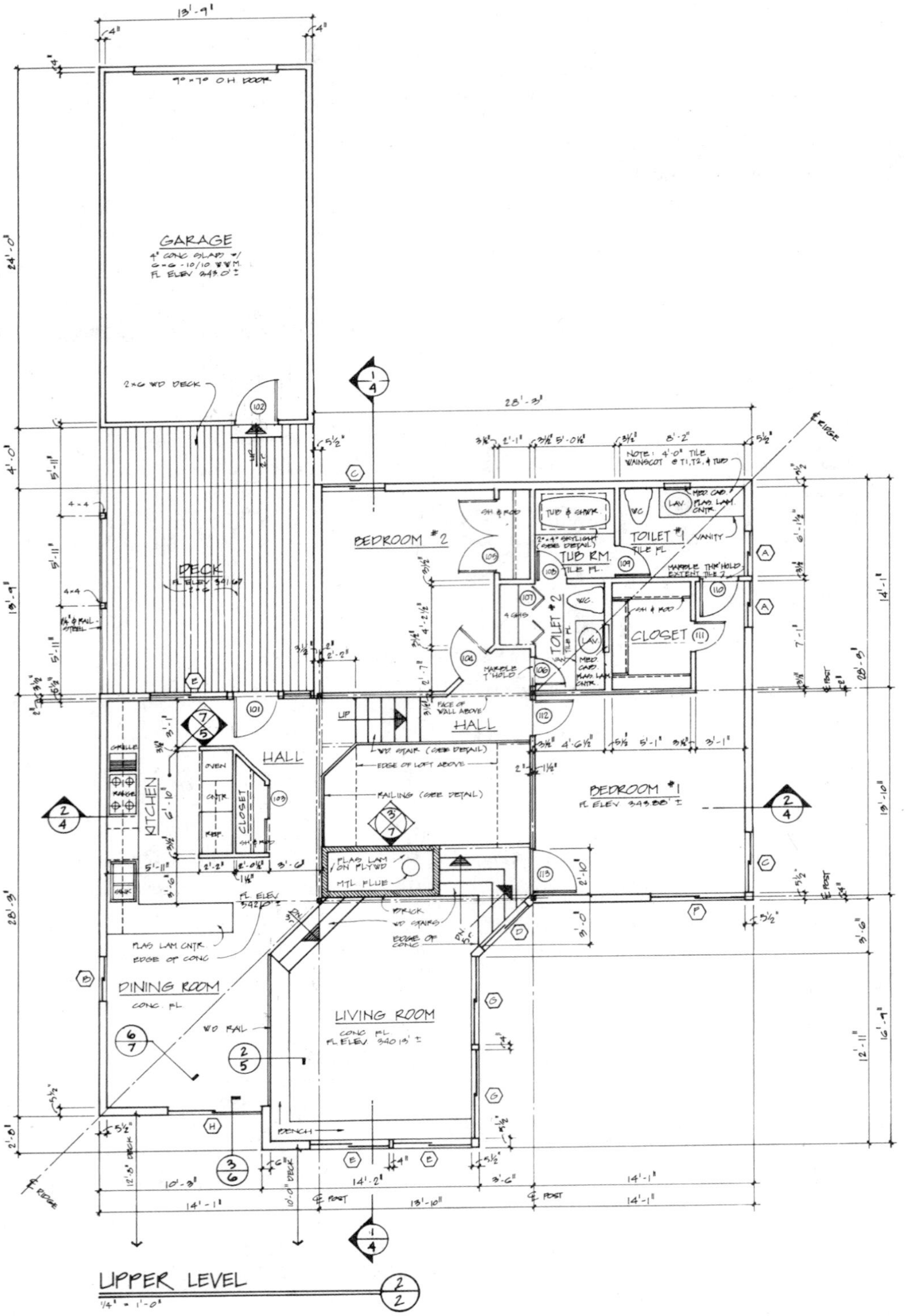

Fig. 1-1 Typical working drawing (Reprinted by permission from Huth, *Understanding Construction Drawings*, Sheet #2. © 1983 by Delmar Publishers Inc.)

agent. This is the *diazo process,* figure 1-2. In this process, the sensitized paper and the original drawing are exposed to a strong light. After exposure, the sensitized paper is exposed to ammonia vapor. No fixing or washing is necessary.

A print made by the diazo process is the reverse of a blueprint. The background is white and the lines are blue.

COMPUTER-AIDED DRAFTING

Many architectural firms and construction companies use computers for design and drafting. A drawing prepared on a computer looks very similar to one prepared manually. The only difference is that the CAD (computer-aided drafting) drawing has more consistent lettering and the overall appearance may be a little neater, figure 1-3.

The advantage of CAD over manual drafting is that in CAD the drawings can be easily revised. If the designer wants to change a single detail, that can be done without having to redraw the entire sheet. Also, the basic outline of the building can be transferred from the first floor plan, to the foundation plan, the second floor plan, the electrical plan, and so on.

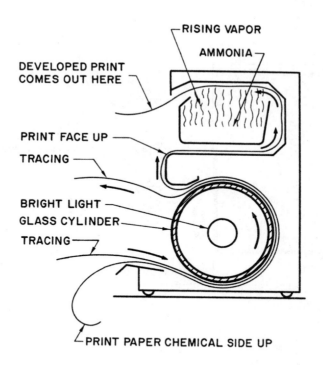

RISING VAPOR

AMMONIA

DEVELOPED PRINT COMES OUT HERE

PRINT FACE UP

TRACING

BRIGHT LIGHT

GLASS CYLINDER

TRACING

PRINT PAPER CHEMICAL SIDE UP

ROLLERS MOVE THE TRACING AND PRINT AROUND THE LIGHT AND MOVE THE PRINT PAST THE RISING AMMONIA VAPOR

Fig. 1-2 The Diazo Process

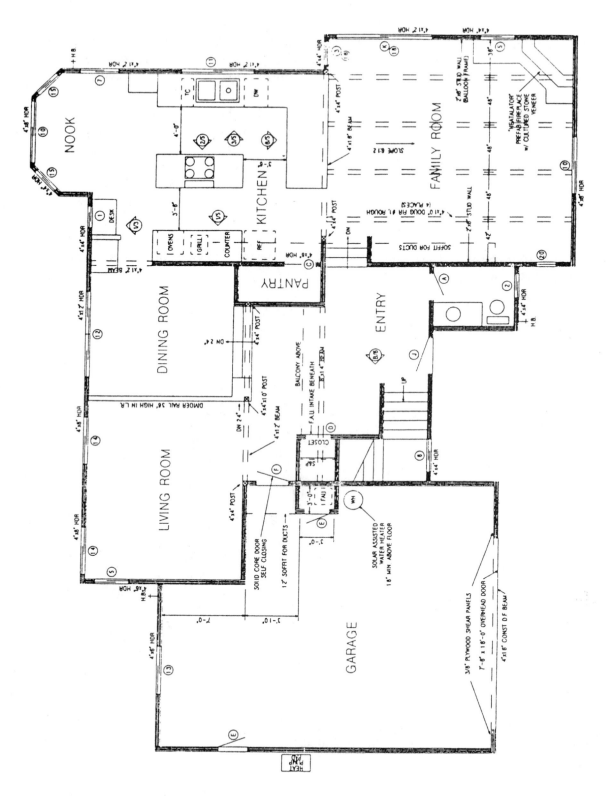

Fig. 1-3 Architectural drawing produced with CAD (Courtesy of Hewlett-Packard Company)

ASSIGNMENT

Questions

1. What is the main purpose of construction drawings? are used for the purpose of communication between the different groups. ex. financers, builders.

2. What three basic characteristics of a building are shown on drawings? The size, shape and location.

3. Why is it important for construction drawings to be made according to established rules? So the will be interpreted the same by everyone.

4. To make blueprints or diazo prints, the original must be on what type of sheet? Sensitized paper Translusant

5. When prints are made from a set of working drawings, where are the originals kept? in the architects or engineers office.

6. What color is the background on a modern print of a construction drawing? white.

7. Briefly describe the diazo process. Translusant the sensitized paper and the original are exposed to a stronglight then exposed to ammonia vapour.

8. What advantages does CAD have over manual drafting methods? You can change little things rather than doing a new drawing.

UNIT 2 Orthographic Projections

OBJECTIVES

After completing this unit, you will be able to:

- visualize the actual shape of an object shown in orthographic projection.

- identify the location of the various views in orthographic projection.

KINDS OF DRAWINGS

There are basically two ways to draw a three-dimensional object on a flat sheet of paper. In *pictorial drawings* the object is drawn like it actually looks. These types of drawings show several sides of an object in one view. This tends to crowd information. Furthermore, to make the drawing look like the object, many angles must be distorted and some lines must be shortened. To communicate information more accurately, working drawings usually use orthographic projection.

In *orthographic projection* two or more views of the object are drawn. Each view shows only one side of the object. The views are always positioned in the same place on the drawing, so the person reading the drawing knows where to find them.

The Glass Box

To illustrate the position of the views, assume that the house in figure 2-1 is suspended inside a hinged glass box, figure 2-2.

Looking in the direction of arrow ①, the front of the house and garage are shown.

In this view, the length and height of the house can be seen.

Looking in the direction of arrow ②, the left end of the house is shown. None of the detail from the main part of the house shows in this left-end view; only the garage.

Looking in the direction of arrow ③, the top of the house is seen. The small rectangle in the middle is the outline of the chimney, which cannot be seen in other views.

What has been done up to this point is to project the views of the building away from the block itself, onto the glass. The three views are still in three separate planes. Since a sheet of drawing paper is all in one plane, the next step is to unfold the three planes of the box so they form one plane. The positions of the three views on the flattened-out glass box are shown in figure 2-3. The picture shows the normal positions of these views on a working drawing or an orthographic projection. When the object shown is as large as a building, it is not always possible to include all of the views on one sheet of paper.

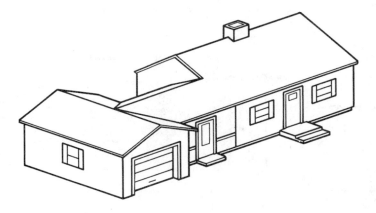

Fig. 2-1 House

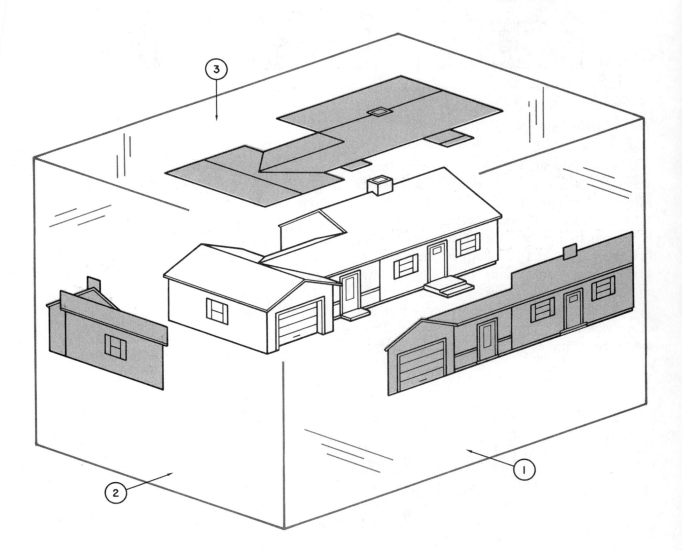

Fig. 2-2 House suspended inside glass box

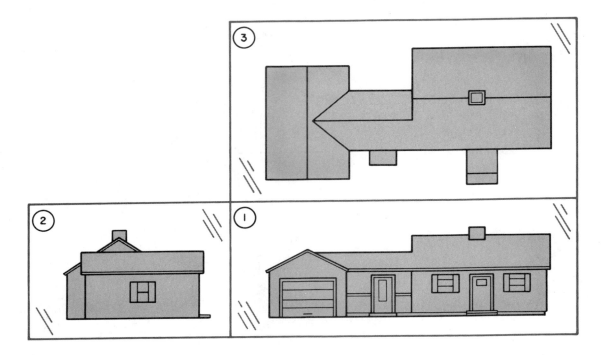

Fig. 2-3 Glass box unfolded

Note the relationship of each of these views to each other. View ③ is located directly above and in line with View ① . Both views have a common width. View ② is located to the left side of and directly in line with View ① . Both of these views share common dimensions, the overall height, and the height of the eaves.

If it is necessary to show an object in other views, the process is the same. The rear view is projected onto the back of the glass box. The left-end view is projected onto the left end of the box. Working drawings produced for the building trades include enough views to show all necessary information. However, it is not considered a good practice to repeat information unnecessarily. Round objects, for example, often require only two views. An additional orthographic view of the plug shown in figure 2-4 would not provide more information.

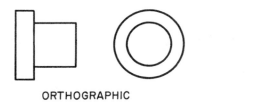

ORTHOGRAPHIC   PICTORIAL

Fig. 2-4 Plug

ASSIGNMENT

Questions

1. Name 2 views in orthographic projection that show the overall length of
    an object. _Views 1 and 3_

2. Name 2 views in orthographic projection that show the overall height of
    an object. _Views 1 and 2_

3. Why is it important for all of the views on a working drawing to be in
    the proper positions? _So the person reading the drawing
    will know where to find them._

For questions 4-8, refer to the drawing of the house.

4. Which line or surface in the top view represents (C) ?   _E_

5. Which line or surface in the right-side view represents (A) ?   _G_

6. Which line or surface in the front view represents (H) ?   _D_

7. Which line or surface in the right-side view represents (B) ?   _J_

8. Which line or surface in the top view represents (I) ?   _F_

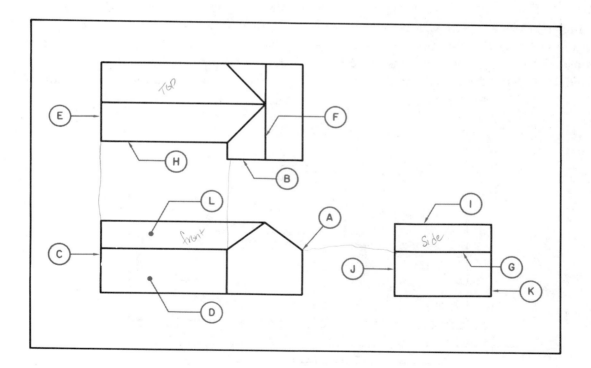

UNIT 3   Plans, Elevations, and Sections

OBJECTIVES

After completing this unit, you will be able to:

- read simple plan views, elevation views, and section views.
- determine the relationship between the various views of a set of working drawings.

PLANS

Working drawings for construction are almost always done by orthographic projection. However, to help identify the views, they are given names. The top view is called a *plan* or *plan view,* figure 3-1. In order to show as much information as possible, plan views are drawn at several points in a building. A typical set of working drawings includes a foundation plan, floor plan, and plot plan.

Where it is necessary to show interior detail, such as on a floor plan, an imaginary cut is made through the building, figure 3-2. For a floor plan, this horizontal cut is made at a height that passes through the windows, doors, and other wall openings. Looking straight down at this imaginary cut, you see the floor plan, figure 3-3. This shows the arrangement of rooms, locations of doors and windows, and other important information.

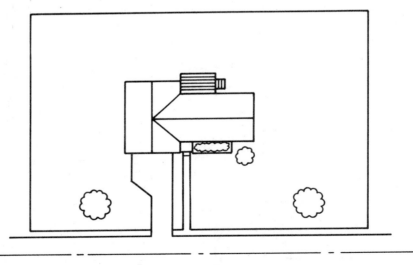

Fig. 3-1 A plot plan is a common type of plan view.

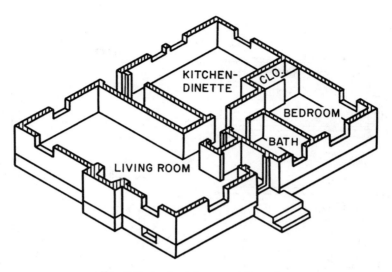

Fig. 3-2 An imaginary cut is made.

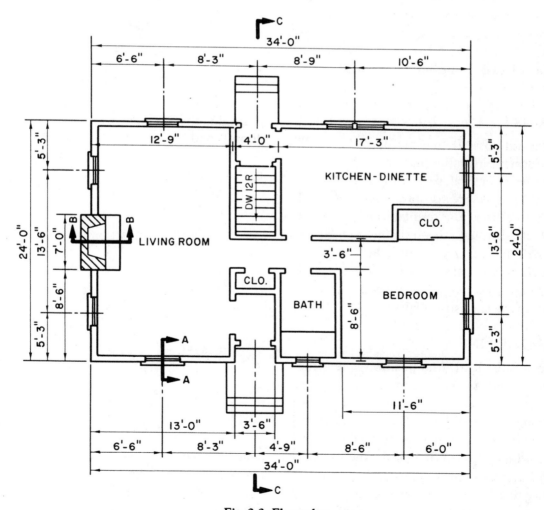

Fig. 3-3 Floor plan

Fig. 3-4 Front elevation

ELEVATIONS

Drawings which show height, such as front views and side views, are called *elevations.* Elevation drawings are named according to their location. A typical set of working drawings includes elevations of each side of the building. Elevations do not show interior detail, figure 3-4.

SECTIONS

It is not possible to show all of the necessary information in the plans and elevations. To see the structural parts of a wall, for example, it is necessary to draw a section view, figure 3-5. This is the result of an imaginary vertical cut through the building, similar to the horizontal cut made for the floor plan. Most section views are vertical, but horizontal (or plan) sections may be included. In section views the parts are usually labeled.

REFERENCE LINES

To locate clearly the position where the structure is cut away to show a section, the drafter uses a *reference line* or *cutting-plane line* through the structure. The reference line has an arrow on each end showing the direction in which the section is to be viewed.

In a drawing that contains many reference lines, the line is identified with letters at each end, such as A-A, B-B, C-C. A typical set of

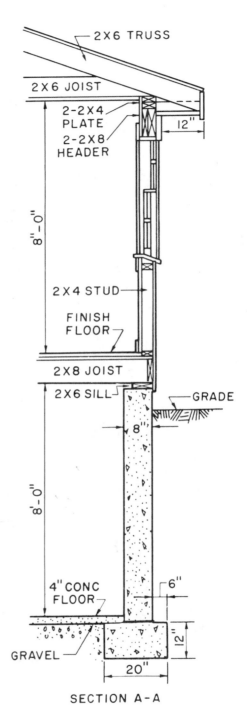

SECTION A-A

Fig. 3-5 Wall section

plans may contain many sections, each identified with the same letters as its corresponding reference line, such as section A-A, section B-B, and section C-C, figure 3-3.

ASSIGNMENT

A.   Questions

1. Which view shows what a person in the illustration would see?

    a. Plan view
    b. Right elevation
    c. Left elevation
    d. Section view

2. Which view shows the location of the kitchen?

    a. Floor plan
    b. Wall section
    c. Front elevation
    d. Side elevation

3. Which view shows the size of the materials used in the walls?

    a. Floor plan
    b. Wall section
    c. Any elevation
    d. Basement plan

4. What is indicated by a heavy line through part of a drawing with an arrowhead and the letter B at each end?

    a. A missing dimension
    b. A window or door
    c. A floor plan
    d. A section view

5. Which view in a set of construction drawings corresponds with the top view in orthographic projection?

    a. Plan
    b. Front elevation
    c. Right-side elevation
    d. Section

6. Which view in a set of construction drawings corresponds with the front view in orthographic projection?

    a. Plan
    b. Front elevation
    c. Right-side elevation
    d. Section

B.   Print Reading

Refer to the drawings in the back of the textbook to answer the following questions.

7. Which sheet includes the building elevation showing the overhead door in the garage? _____ 3/6 x 4/6 _____

✓8. Which view shows the most detail about the construction of the kitchen roof? _____ Section View   6/6 _____

9. On which drawing would you find the length and width of bedroom #1? _____ 3/6   Floor Plan _____

✓10. On which drawings (there are more than one) can you find the overall length of the building? _____ 3/6, 1/6, 2/6 & 4/6 _____
Foundations , Floor , Plot Plan

11. How many plan views are included? (Count the drawings, not the sheets.) _____ 4   Sht# (1, 2, 3, 6) _____

12. How many exterior elevation views are included? _____ 2 x 4   sht# 4,5 _____

13. On what sheet or sheets are the section views shown? _____ 6/6 _____

14. What kinds of drawings are used to show the fireplace details? _____
Cross Section , Plan , Sectional, elevation (front)

UNIT 4   Dimensioning

OBJECTIVES

After completing this unit, you will be able to:

- identify dimensions on a drawing.
- read an architect's scale.

BASIC DIMENSIONING

Dimensions are included on a drawing to show the size and location of all parts. The methods of showing the necessary dimensions are standardized to insure uniform interpretation. The sketch of the wall in figure 4-1 shows an accepted form of dimensioning.

The *extension lines* that show what is dimensioned are a continuation of the lines of the object itself. To avoid confusion between the object lines and the extension lines, a short break occurs between them. For further distinction, the object lines are drawn fairly thick, while the extension lines are drawn thin but sharp enough to be distinct.

The *dimension line* is drawn at right angles to the extension lines. It extends from one extension line to the other. The weight of this line is the same as that of the extension line — thin, but sharp and distinct. The arrowheads

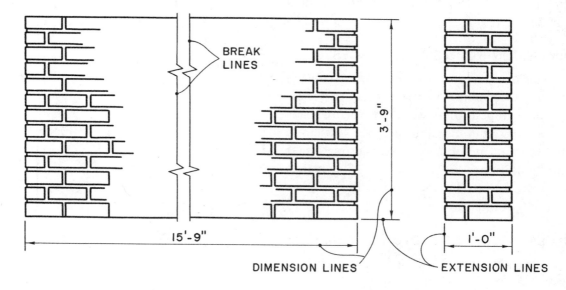

Fig. 4-1 Extension and dimension lines in use

at each end of this line are used to clearly show the beginning and ending points of the dimension. These arrowheads are all drawn to a uniform size and are usually made about three times as long as they are wide. Some drawings are dimensioned using slashes or ticks at the ends of the dimension lines, figure 4-2.

When long objects must be shown in a small space, *break lines* are used, figure 4-1. Break lines indicate that the entire length has not been drawn. Dimension lines are not broken when break lines are used.

Dimensions are given in feet and inches, for example, 6'-8" or 1'-3". Even those dimensions that are full feet with no inches are dimensioned in this manner. Typical dimensions of this type are 6'-0", 2'-0", and 12'-0". This is done to eliminate the possibility of a mistake because of not understanding a dimension. Exceptions to this rule are those dimensions that are standards of construction, such as the center-to-center distance of studs, joists, or rafters. This distance is given in inches as in 24" OC (On Center), 16" OC, or 16" CC (Center to Center). Also on some drawings where most dimensions are less than one foot, the inch marks are left off.

DIMENSIONING IN SMALL PLACES

In many instances, the space between the two extension lines is too small to permit drawing a dimension line with two arrowheads and a printed dimension. Figure 4-3 shows the accepted methods of dimensioning under such conditions. In all cases, the dimensions are placed outside the object lines rather than within the drawing.

DIMENSIONING STRUCTURAL MEMBERS

On any set of drawings, dimensions serve two important functions: to indicate the location of a specific construction feature

and to indicate size. In architectural drawing, extension and dimension lines are used to show overall building sizes and locate building features.

The structural parts themselves are usually dimensioned for size. A line with an arrowhead that leads from a clear space where dimensions or notes are written to the structural member is called a *leader*. Figure 4-4, shows a typical example of this form of dimensioning.

Because of the greatly reduced size of the drawing, most structural members appear very small and would be extremely difficult

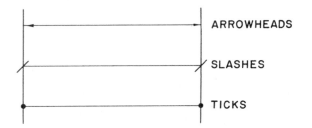

Fig. 4-2 Three forms of dimensioning

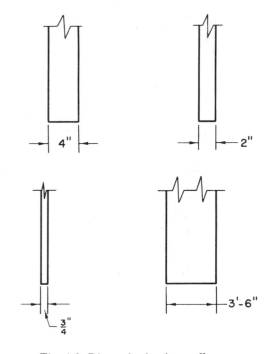

Fig. 4-3 Dimensioning in small spaces

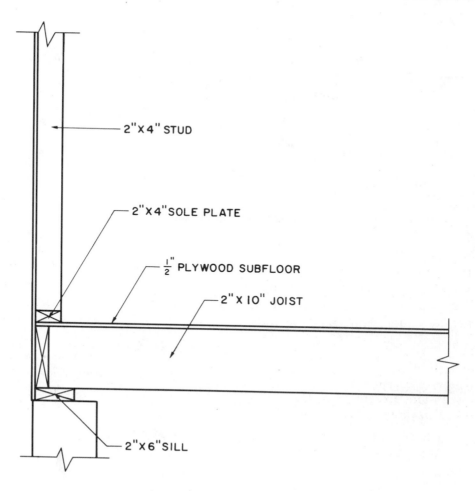

Fig. 4-4 Leaders used on a drawing

to dimension if extension and dimension lines were used in the standard manner. Also, moving the dimension to a clear space permits the architect to include other important information. In figure 4-4, the dimension for each structural part includes the name and purpose of the part. Note, for example, the dimension 1/2" plywood subfloor. In addition to the size, this dimension contains a description of the kind of material used and its purpose in the construction.

CHAIN DIMENSIONS

It is often necessary to show location dimensions of several construction features in a straight line. These are normally shown with

dimensions from one feature to the next. Dimensions chained together this way are called *chain dimensions*. The total of a chain of dimensions should equal the overall dimension, if one is given. In figure 4-5, the chain dimensions are 5'-7", 5'-7", 6'-8", 5'-7", and 5'-7". This chain adds up to 29'-0", the overall dimension shown.

NOMINAL MATERIAL SIZES

Many materials are manufactured to slightly different sizes than their stated sizes. For example, a 2 x 4 piece of lumber actually measures 1 1/2 inches by 3 1/2 inches, and an 8 x 8 x 16 concrete masonry unit actually measures 7 5/8 inches by 7 5/8 inches by

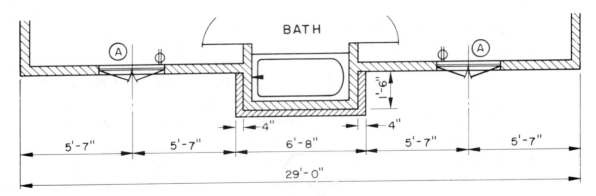

Fig. 4-5 Chain dimensions

15 5/8 inches. The stated size (2x4 or 8x8x16) is called the *nominal size*. On small-scale drawings, such as floor plans and building elevations, materials are usually drawn to their nominal size. However, on large-scale details, they are sometimes drawn to their actual sizes. Therefore, it is possible that a piece of material will be shown a slightly different size than its stated or nominal size.

ASSIGNMENT

A. Questions

1. What are the two types of information about a part that can be shown by dimensions? _Size & Location_

2. What is the purpose of the extension lines used at the ends of dimension lines? _Continuation of the lines of the object itself._

3. How would a dimension be written for a part that is three feet, four and one-half inches long? _3'-4½"_

4. What is meant by nominal size? _The size by which the material is specified, the actual size is usually smaller._

5. How are the nominal sizes of parts shown when it is not practical to include them with normal dimension and extension lines? _Use a leader line & a Note_

B. Print Reading
Refer to the drawings in the back of the book.

6. According to the floor plan, what are the overall outside dimensions of the building? _67'-0" x 48'-6" sht. #1,2_

7. According to the floor plan, what is the length of the closet in bedroom #1? _4'-6"_

8. According to the floor plan, what is the length of the porch? _____
   _____ Sht. # 3 _____ 16'-0"

9. According to the fireplace details, what is the height of the fireplace opening? _____ 2'-6" _____

10. According to the typical wall section, what are the nominal dimensions of the wall studs? _____ 1-2" _____ x _____ 4" _____

11. According to the Section Thru Kitchen Roof, how thick is the insulation between the ceiling joists? _____ 6" _____

12. What is the total of the chain of dimensions shown inside the excavated portion of the basement? _____ 29'-0 - 29'-6" _____

13. According to the Foundation Plan, what are the dimensions of the fireplace foundation? _____ 2'-10" _____ x _____ 7'-6" _____

14. On the Foundation Plan, what is the width of the opening in the foundation for the overhead door in the garage? _____ 18' _____

15. According to the Site Plan, what are the overall dimensions of the garage? _____ 22'-0" _____ x _____ 25'-6" _____

UNIT 5   Scales

OBJECTIVES

After completing this unit, you will be able to:

- read an architect's scale.
- use a scale on architectural drawings.

SCALE DRAWINGS

Construction work is usually too large to be drawn to actual size on a drawing sheet. This requires drawing everything proportionately smaller. All dimensions should be clearly indicated on the prints, and dimensions should not be scaled for the purpose of construction or estimating. However, there are times when it is useful to get a rough idea of the size or location of an object by scaling. *Scaling* means to measure distances with an architect's scale.

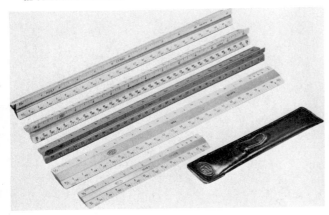

Fig. 5-1 Architects triangular scales
(Courtesy of Teledyne Post)

READING AN ARCHITECT'S SCALE

The architect's scale is *open divided*, figure 5-1. This means the scales have the main units undivided and a fully subdivided, extra unit placed at the zero end of the scales.

Listed below are eleven scales found on the architect's triangular scale:

Full scale
3/32" = 1'- 0"
1/8" = 1'- 0"
3/16" = 1'- 0"
1/4" = 1'- 0"
3/8" = 1'- 0"
1/2" = 1'- 0"
3/4" = 1'- 0"
1" = 1'- 0"
1 1/2" = 1'- 0"
3" = 1'- 0"

Two scales are combined on each face, except the full-size scale which is fully divided into sixteenths. The combined scales work together because one is twice as large as the other, and their zero points and extra divided units are on opposite ends of the scale.

Architectural drawings use feet and inches as the major units of measurement. The architect's scale is broken down into these units in reduced scales. This is done so that large buildings and details can be drawn on paper. This makes the drawings smaller and easier to handle.

The fraction, or number, near the zero at each end of the scale indicates the unit length in inches that is used on the drawing to represent one foot of the actual building. The extra unit near the zero end of the scale is subdivided into twelfths of a foot, or inches, as well as fractions of inches on the larger scales.

1/4″ = 1′-0″ Scale

Most house plans and small buildings are drawn to the 1/4 inch equals one foot scale. This means that each quarter of an inch on the drawing equals one foot of the actual size of the building. For example, a line drawn 3 inches long represents 12 feet on the building. The scale of the drawing is noted on the drawing and is usually given in the title box on each drawing. Sometimes when special details are given, the scale is placed directly under the detail.

To read the architect's triangular scale, turn it to the 1/4-inch scale. The scale is divided on the left from the zero towards the 1/4 mark so that each line represents one inch. Counting the marks from the zero toward the 1/4 mark, there are twelve lines marked on the scale. Each one of these lines is one inch on the 1/4″ = 1′-0″ scale. To the left of

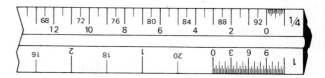

Fig. 5-2

the zero and inch-divided section in figure 5-1, notice there are two sets of numerals. One set starts at 92 and gets smaller as you move away from the zero. The other set starts with 2 and gets larger. The set of numerals that gets larger indicates feet at the 1/4″ = 1′-0″ scale. Between every printed even number is an unnumbered line to indicate the odd number of feet. Therefore, the first line to the left of the 92 in figure 5-2 indicates one foot. The number to the left of the 80 (halfway between the larger printed 6 and 8) represents 7 feet.

1/8″ = 1′-0″ Scale

The fraction 1/8 is on the opposite end of the same scale, figure 5-3. This is the 1/8-inch scale and is read from the right to the left. Notice that the divided unit is only half as large as the one on the 1/4-inch end of the scale. Counting the lines from zero toward the 1/8 mark, there are only six lines. This means that each line represents two inches at the 1/8-inch scale. Graduations for feet are similar to those on the 1/4″ = 1′-0″ scale.

1 1/2″ = 1′-0″ Scale

Now look at the 1 1/2-inch scale, figure 5-4. The divided unit is broken into twelfths of an inch and also a fractional part of an inch.

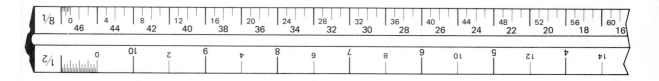

Fig. 5-3

Reading from the zero toward the number 1 1/2, notice the numerals 3, 6, and 9. These numerals represent the measurements of 3 inches, 6 inches, and 9 inches at the 1 1/2″ = 1′-0″ scale. From the zero to the first long mark that represents one inch (which is the same length as the mark shown at 3) are 4 lines. This means that each line on the scale is equal to 1/4 of an inch. Reading the zero to the 3, read each line as follows: 1/4, 1/2, 3/4, 1, 1 1/4, 1 1/2, 1 3/4, 2, 2 1/4, 2 1/2, 2 3/4, and 3 inches.

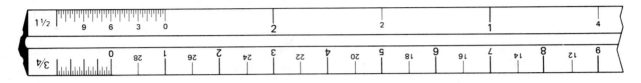

Fig. 5-4

ASSIGNMENT

A.   Reading Scales

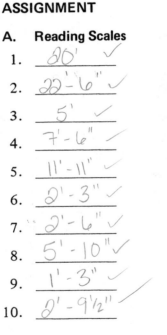

1. _____ 80′ ✓
2. _____ 22′-6″ ✓
3. _____ 5′ ✓
4. _____ 7′-6″ ✓
5. _____ 11′-11″ ✓
6. _____ 2′-3″ ✓
7. _____ 2′-6″ ✓
8. _____ 5′-10″ ✓
9. _____ 1′-3″ ✓
10. _____ 2′-9½″ ✓

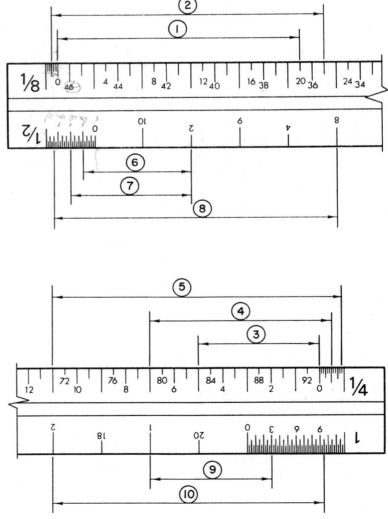

B. Scaling Drawings

Use an architect's scale to measure the following items from the drawings in the back of the textbook.

11. Overall height of the chimney at its centerline on sheet 4/6. _23'8" 19.2'_

12. Width of the cellar window, including its frame, on sheet 4/6. _2'-10"_

13. Length of the tub in the bath between bedrooms 2 and 3, sheet 3/6. _5'-0"_

14. Width of the hall, between the walls, in the bedroom area, sheet 3/6. _3'-1"_

15. Length of the front porch, sheet 3/6. _16'-2"_

16. Height of the door, not including the frame, on the left end of the right elevation, sheet 5/6. _6'-6"_

17. Length of the 2 x 4 brace in the Section Thru Kitchen Roof, sheet 6/6. _1'1"_

18. Length of the pipe column in the Stair Section, sheet 6/6. _8'_

19. Depth of the concrete footing in the Typical Wall Section, sheet 6/6. _7½"_

20. Total thickness of the main floor in the Typical Wall Section, sheet 6/6. _10½'_

C. Drawing to Scale

Using an architect's scale draw the following straight lines on a separate sheet of paper.

Scale	Length
1/8″ = 1'-0″	49'-4″
1/4″ = 1'-0″	11'-7″
1/2″ = 1'-0″	8'-3 1/2″
3/8″ = 1'-0″	12'-9″
3/4″ = 1'-0″	4'-2 1/4″
1 1/2″ = 1'-0″	2'-3 5/8″

UNIT 6   Hidden Edges

OBJECTIVES

After completing this unit, you will be able to:

- explain the importance of showing hidden edges on a working drawing.
- indicate a hidden edge on a working drawing.

HIDDEN LINES

In construction work many of the important surfaces and edges are hidden from view. Since these surfaces and edges are important if the instructions are to be complete, it is necessary to show them in the working drawing. To avoid confusion with the visible surfaces and edges which are shown by object lines, the hidden edges are represented by a line of dashes, figure 6-1.

This line of dashes is drawn slightly thinner than the object lines so that it does not detract from the basic shape of the outline. It is still drawn considerably heavier than the extension and dimension lines. Care should be taken to make the dashes a uniform length. There should also be an approximately uniform space between dashes. Otherwise, this type of line will be confused with broken lines used for other purposes.

The concrete block shown in figure 6-1 is an excellent example of how a hidden line is used on a working drawing. If the front view were drawn as we see it, the rectangular holes would not be shown. Without hidden lines, there would be no way to know whether the holes go all the way through the block or stop in the middle. Figure 6-2 shows the second possibility. The addition of the hidden lines to the front view shows the depth of the holes clearly.

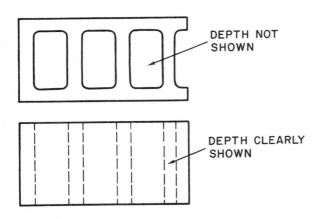

DEPTH NOT SHOWN

DEPTH CLEARLY SHOWN

Fig. 6-1 Hidden lines

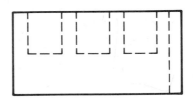

Fig. 6-2 Block with holes only halfway through

DIMENSIONING HIDDEN EDGES

Wherever possible, the dimensions are shown on the view that contains the visible edge lines. This practice is followed because it is easier to interpret. Figure 6-3 illustrates the preferred practice.

All hidden edges and surfaces which are important to understand the drawing should be shown. In some instances there are so many hidden lines that the drawing becomes confusing. To simplify the drawing, the accepted practice is to show the view with a minimum of hidden lines. A section drawing is added to clarify the actual construction features, figure 6-4.

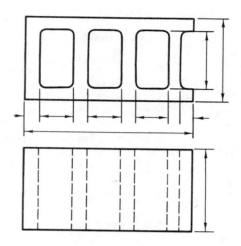

Fig. 6-3 Preferred dimensioning

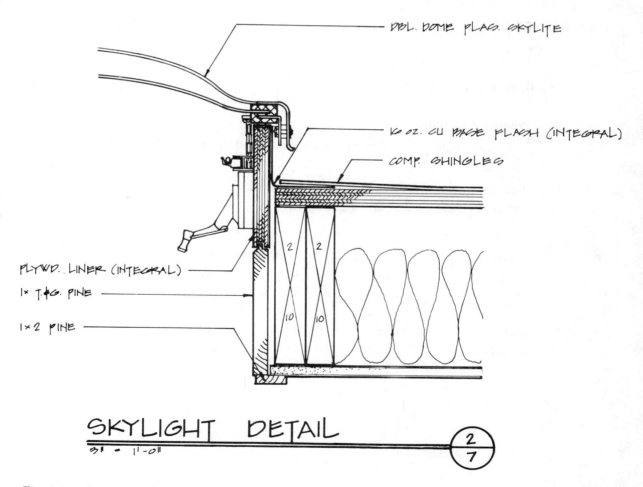

SKYLIGHT DETAIL

3' = 1'-0"

2/7

Fig. 6-4 A drawing of this skylight would require dozens of hidden lines without this section view. (Reprinted by permission from Huth, *Understanding Construction Drawings*, sheet 7. © 1983 by Delmar Publishers Inc.)

ASSIGNMENT

A. Blueprint Reading.

Refer to the drawing of the cabinet.

1. What line in the side view represents (A) ? _K_

2. What line in the front view represents (B) ? _H_

3. What line in the side view represents (C) ? _L_

4. What line in the side view represents (E) ? _P_

5. What is dimension (H) ? _3/8"_

6. What is the thickness of the part indicated by (I) ? _3/4"_

7. What line in the front view represents (D) ? _I_

8. What is dimension (J) ? _7"_

9. What line in the front view represents (F) ? _Q_

10. What line in the front view represents surface (R) ? _N_

11. What line in the side view represents surface (R) ? _G_

B. Blueprint Reading

Refer to the drawings in the back of the textbook to answer the following questions.

12. What is indicated by the dashed lines near the top of sheet 2/6, labeled Furnace Flue? _Ash Pit_

13. What is indicated by the dashed vertical lines in the lower right corner of sheet 4/6? _Extensions of the underground (Wall) support Beams_

14. What is indicated by the pair of dashed horizontal lines across the bottom of the right half of the left elevation? _fondation footing_

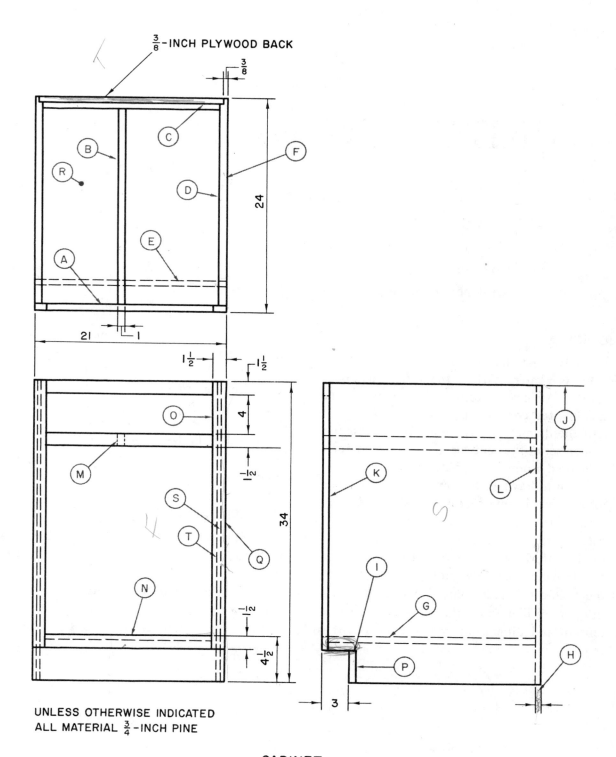

⅜-INCH PLYWOOD BACK

CABINET

UNLESS OTHERWISE INDICATED
ALL MATERIAL ¾-INCH PINE

UNIT 7   Circles and Arcs

OBJECTIVES

After completing this unit, you will be able to:

- show how circles and arcs are drawn.
- use standard dimensioning practice for circles and arcs.

CIRCLES

The first step in drawing a circle is to locate its center. When the center has been located, the circle is drawn with a compass. To do this, the compass is set to the *radius* (one-half the diameter). The point of the compass is then set at the center mark, and the compass is pivoted around this point to draw the circle.

On a drawing, the center of a circle is indicated by the intersection of two centerlines. These lines are used solely for the accurate location and construction of the circle. While these centerlines are important to understand the drawing, they must not be confused with the visible or hidden lines. A centerline is a thin, sharp line about the same weight as extension and dimension lines, figure 7-1. It is made up of long dashes broken with single short dashes.

Circular objects can usually be shown completely in two views; the front and the side. A top view would be a duplication of the side and is, therefore, unnecessary. In order that centerlines are not confused as part of the object, they are normally drawn beyond the object lines.

DIMENSIONING CIRCLES

Centerlines are also used to dimension the location of the center of a circle, figure 7-2.

The circles themselves are dimensioned as shown in figure 7-3, A through D. Method A is used when there is not enough room to

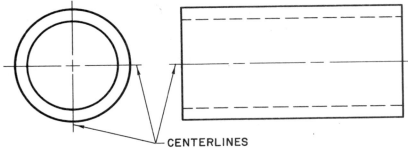

CENTERLINES

Fig. 7-1 Centerlines

28

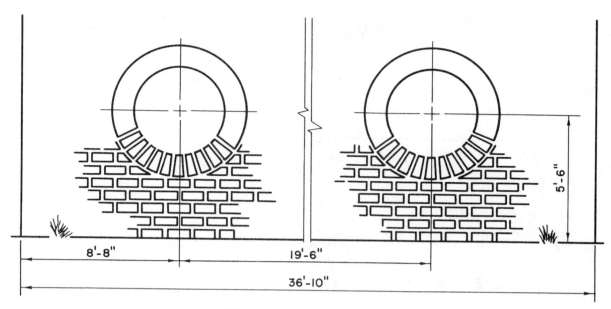

Fig. 7-2 Dimensioning circles

crowd the dimension line, arrows, dimensions, and centerlines within the circle. Method B is used for dimensioning large circles. The dimension line is drawn at an angle to avoid overlapping a centerline. Note that the diameter of the circle — not the radius — is

always used for dimensioning purposes. Method C is used to dimension cylinders. As shown by Method D, when several circles are shown, they are usually located by dimensions that are given from the center of one circle to the center of the next.

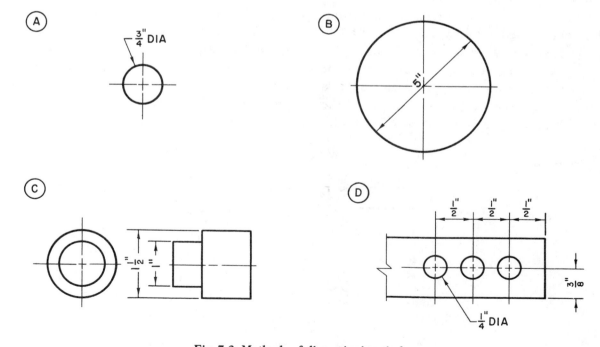

Fig. 7-3 Methods of dimensioning circles

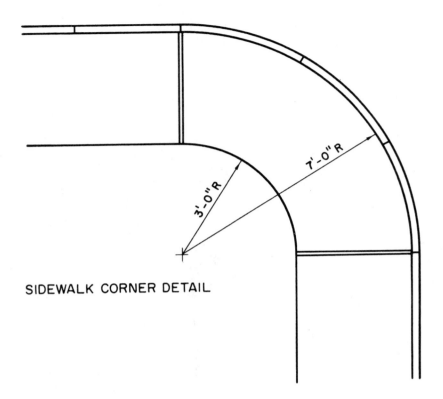

SIDEWALK CORNER DETAIL

Fig. 7-4 Arcs in construction

DRAWING AND DIMENSIONING ARCS

An *arc* is a part of a circle or an incomplete circle. Figure 7-4 shows a typical application of arcs in sidewalk construction.

Like circles, arcs are located by their center points. Dimensions are given from this point for both the location and the size of the arc. The major difference is that the arc di-

mension is given as a radius, and the circle dimension is given as a diameter.

The accepted methods of dimensioning the size of an arc are shown in figure 7-5. The dimension line is run at an angle from the intersection of the centerlines to the arc. Only one arrow is used, touching the object line or arc.

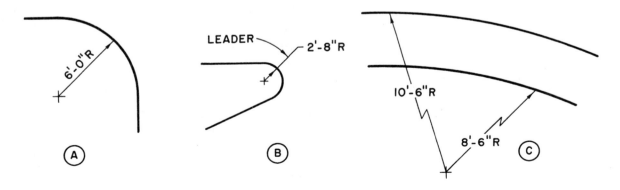

Fig. 7-5 Dimensioning arcs

On the small radius arc at B, a leader is used for the dimension. Although the dimension itself is printed outside of the object, only one arrow is used.

To dimension an arc with a very large radius, as shown at C, frequently requires that the dimension line be run through other parts of the drawing. To avoid possible confusion, the dimension line is started at the intersection of the centerlines, discontinued where it passes through the other details, and started again near the arc. Many drafters and architects use a zigzag in the dimension line to indicate that it has been broken along its length.

BREAK LINES

The methods of showing break lines in cylindrical and rectangular objects vary as shown in figure 7-6.

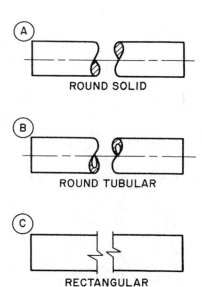

Fig. 7-6 Break lines

ASSIGNMENT

Blueprint Reading.

Refer to the drawing of the lockset mortise.

1. Which lines in the right-side view represent hole (A) ? _____

2. Which lines in the front (left-side) view represent hole (B) ? _____

3. What is dimension (C) ? _____

4. Which surface in the right-side view represents (F) ? _____

5. Which surface in the right-side view represents (M) ? _____

6. What is dimension (N) ? _____

7. What is the radius of the corners at (X) ? _____

8. What is dimension (Y) ? _____

9. What is dimension (U) ? _____

10. What is dimension (Z) ? _____

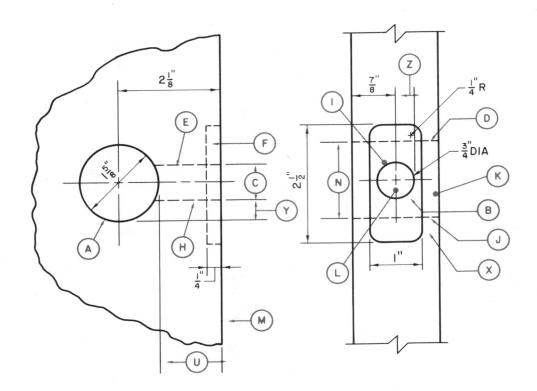

LOCKSET MORTISE

UNIT 8 Symbols, Abbreviations, and Notes

OBJECTIVES

After completing this unit, you will be able to:

- interpret common symbols found on drawings.
- explain the importance of notes on drawings.
- interpret common abbreviations.

SYMBOLS

In order for the architect, engineer, or drafter to make drawings useful, there must be a way to illustrate materials. The simple outline of an object shows its shape. It does not indicate whether it is made of steel, concrete, or wood.

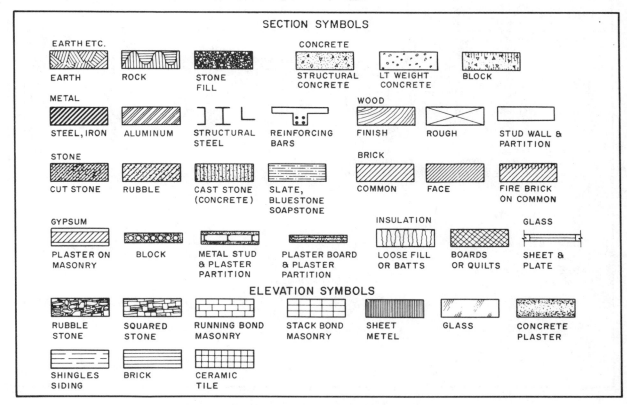

Fig. 8-1 **Symbols found on architectural drawings**

To show materials, the drafter uses symbols. There are two generally accepted sets of material symbols. One set is used on plan and section views. The other set is used on elevations. Figure 8-1 shows the most common material symbols.

In addition to showing materials, symbols are used to show objects that would require too much detail if drawn in a conventional way. These objects include plumbing fixtures, electric fixtures, and some mechanical devices, figure 8-2.

The symbols shown in this unit are only a sampling of the most frequently used symbols. There are many references available that show more complete lists of conventional symbols. Also, many drafters and architects include a key to the symbols they have used someplace in the set of working drawings.

ABBREVIATIONS

Many words or phrases are standard in the construction language. To eliminate the need for writing these out every time they are used, standard abbreviations are used, figure 8-3.

NOTES

Although drawings are used to illustrate graphically how a structure is to be built, not all information can be shown with lines, symbols, and dimensions. Notes are added to drawings to explain items that cannot be readily drawn. Notes are not used, however,

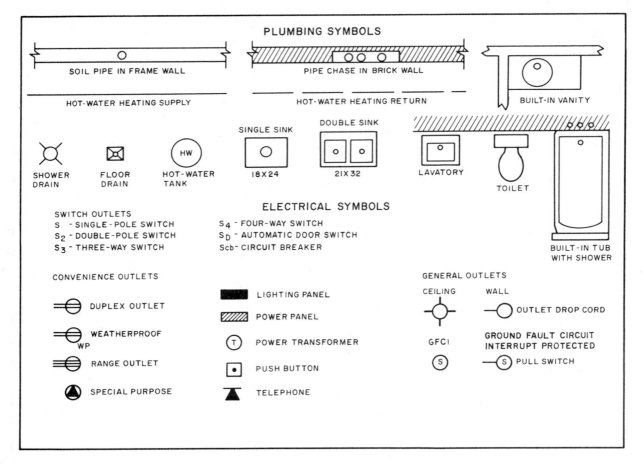

Fig. 8-2 Mechanical and electrical symbols

AWG	American Wire Gage	GYP	Gypsum
AMP or A	Ampere	HB	Hose Bibb
APVD	Approved	HD	Head
ASPH	Asphalt	HDWD	Hardwood
ASSY	Assembly	HW	Hot Water
B	Bathroom	ID	Inside Diameter
BD	Board	INSUL	Insulation
BLDG	Building	INTR	Interior
BLK	Block	KD	Kiln Dried
BLT	Bolt	KIT	Kitchen
BM	Beam, Bench Mark, or Board Measure	LBR	Lumber
BOT	Bottom	LG	Length
BR	Bedroom	LNTL	Lintel
BRK	Brick	MATL	Material
BSMT	Basement	MFR	Manufacturer
BTU	British Thermal Unit	MLDG	Molding
CB	Circuit Breaker	MSNRY	Masonry
CCB	Concrete Block	NOM	Nominal
CFM	Cubic Feet Per Minute	OC	On Center
CI	Cast Iron	OD	Outside Diameter
CL or ℄	Centerline	PC	Piece
CLG	Ceiling	PLMB	Plumbing
CLO	Closet	PLY WD	Plywood
COL	Column	PN	Part Number
CONC	Concrete	PNT	Paint
CSG	Casing	R	Radius
C to C	Center to Center	REINF	Reinforced
CU YD	Cubic Yard	RM	Room
DBL	Double	RTN	Return
DIA	Diameter	SDG	Siding
DR	Dining Room	SEW	Sewer
DWL	Dowel	SHTHG	Sheathing
ENTR	Entrance	SPEC	Specification
EQL SP	Equally Spaced	SQ FT	Square Foot
EXC	Excavate or Except	STD	Standard
EXT	Exterior or Extinguisher	SURF	Surface
FD	Floor Drain	SUSP	Suspend
FDN	Foundation	T & G	Tongue and Groove
FL	Floor	THK	Thick
FLG	Flooring	UNFIN	Unfinished
FNSH	Finish	V	Volt
FTG	Fitting or Footing	W	Watt
GA	Gage	WD	Wood
GALVI	Galvanized Iron	WH	Water Heater
GAR	Garage	WI	Wrought Iron
GL	Glass	YD	Yard
GR	Grade		

Fig. 8-3 Commonly used abbreviations

to replace complete and detailed drawings. Notes should be easily understood by all who will read the drawings. Notice that in figure 8-4, the notes are easy to understand without prior knowledge of the building.

General notes, those which apply to many parts of the structure, are neatly lettered in an open area of the drawing. Notes that explain a specific part of the construction are keyed to that point with a leader.

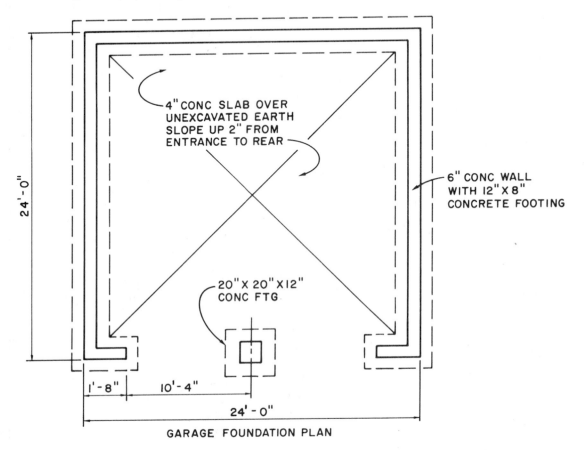

4" CONC SLAB OVER UNEXCAVATED EARTH SLOPE UP 2" FROM ENTRANCE TO REAR

6" CONC WALL WITH 12" X 8" CONCRETE FOOTING

20" X 20" X 12" CONC FTG

24'- 0"

1'- 8"   10'- 4"

24'- 0"

GARAGE FOUNDATION PLAN

Fig. 8-4 Typical notes on drawings

ASSIGNMENT

A. Questions

Write the abbreviation for each of the following:

1. Building BLDG
2. Concrete CONC
3. Plywood PLY WD
4. Exterior EXT
5. Interior INTR

6. On center OC
7. Foundation FDN
8. Wood WD
9. Insulation INSUL
10. Cubic yards CU YD

B.   Identification. Refer to the drawings of the fireplace on this page and page 38.

What material is indicated by each of the following:

A   ROUGH wood   F   Brick/Common

B   finish WD   G   CONC w/Rebar

C   Struct steel   H   Earth

D   fire brick   I   Brick

E   concrete   J   slate

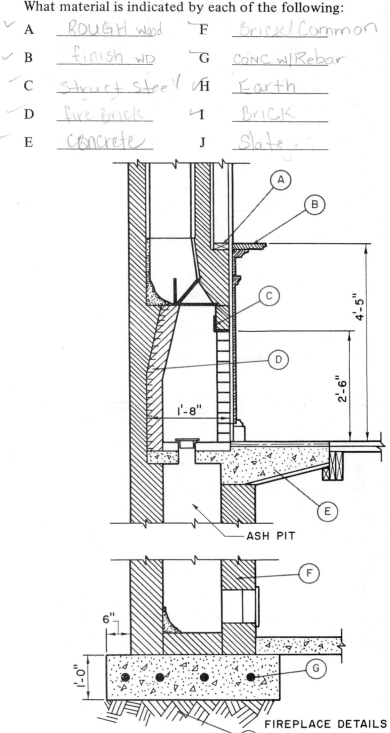

ASH PIT

FIREPLACE DETAILS

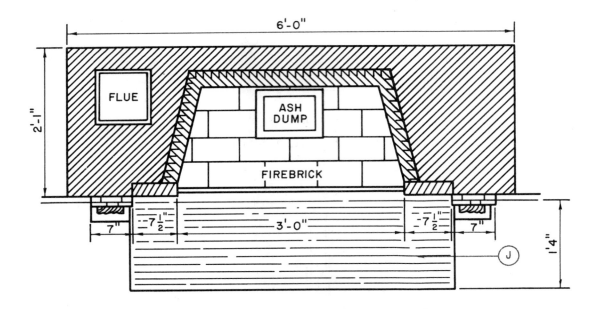

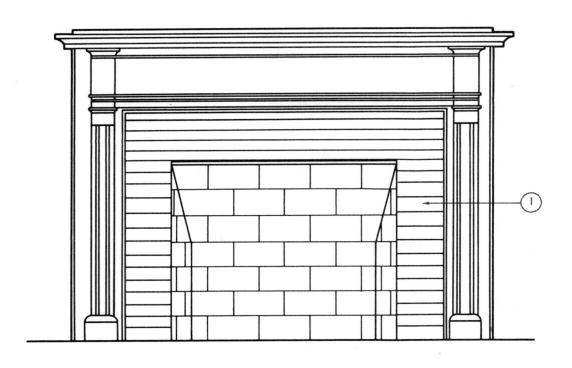

C. Blueprint Reading.

Refer to the drawings in the back of the textbook to answer these questions.

11. On what drawings are ceiling light fixtures shown? ✓ 2,3/6

12. How many toilets are in the house? ✓ 2

13. On what drawing is the lighting panel shown? ✓ 2/6

14. What material is shown on the front elevation between the two bedroom windows? Squared Stone/Wood

15. What material is used on the outside of the fireplace? Face Brick

16. How many pieces of window glass are shown on the right-side elevation? 18

17. What fill material is used under the slab? gravel

18. On what drawing is the earth symbol used? Jdie/Fire Place

19. Of what material is the fireplace mantle shelf made? WD (finished)

20. According to the typical wall section, what 6-inch material is between the rafters? Insulation

Section 2
Math for Construction

UNIT 9 Fractions and Mixed Numbers

OBJECTIVES

After completing this unit, you will be able to:

- add, subtract, multiply, and divide common fractions.
- add, subtract, multiply, and divide mixed numbers.
- add, subtract, multiply, and divide combinations of fractions, mixed numbers, and whole numbers.

DEFINITIONS

In any area of study it is necessary to know the language before you can learn to work in that area. To learn the mathematics of construction, you must understand the language of mathematics as well as the language of construction.

- A *fraction* is a value which shows the number of equal parts taken of a whole quantity. A fraction consists of a numerator and a denominator.

$$\frac{7}{16} \begin{array}{l} \leftarrow\text{Numerator} \\ \leftarrow\text{Denominator} \end{array}$$

- *Equivalent fractions* are fractions which have the same value. The value of a fraction is **not** changed by multiplying the numerator and denominator by the same number.

   Example Express $\frac{5}{8}$ as thirty-seconds.

$$\frac{5}{8} = \frac{?}{32}$$

Determine what number the denominator is multiplied by to get the desired denominator. $(32 \div 8 = 4)$

Multiply the numerator and denominator by 4.

$$\frac{5}{8} \times \frac{4}{4} = \frac{20}{32}$$

- The *lowest common denominator* of two or more fractions is the smallest denominator which is evenly divisible by each of the denominators of the fractions.

   Example 1 The lowest common denominator of $\frac{3}{4}, \frac{5}{8}$, and $\frac{13}{32}$ is 32, because 32 is the smallest number evenly divisible by 4, 8, and 32.

$$32 \div 4 = 8$$
$$32 \div 8 = 4$$
$$32 \div 32 = 1$$

   Example 2 The lowest common denominator of $\frac{2}{3}, \frac{1}{5}$, and $\frac{7}{10}$ is 30, because 30 is the smallest number evenly divisible by 3, 5, and 10.

$$30 \div 3 = 10$$
$$30 \div 5 = 6$$
$$30 \div 10 = 3$$

- *Factors* are numbers used in mutliplying. For example, 3 and 5 are factors of 15.

$$3 \times 5 = 15$$

- A fraction is in its *lowest terms* when the numerator and the denominator do not contain a common factor.

   Example Express $\frac{12}{16}$ in lowest terms.

   Determine the largest common factor in the numerator and denominator. The numerator and the denominator can be evenly divided by 4.

$$\frac{12 \div 4}{16 \div 4} = \frac{3}{4}$$

- A *mixed number* is a whole number plus a fraction.

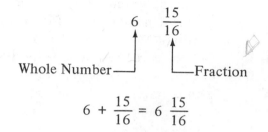

Whole Number ⎯⎯⎯⎯⎯⎯⎯⎯⎯⎯ Fraction

$$6 + \frac{15}{16} = 6\frac{15}{16}$$

- *Expressing fractions as mixed numbers.* In certain fractions, the numerator is larger than the denominator. To express the fraction as a mixed number, divide the numerator by the denominator. Express the fractonal part in lowest terms.

   Example Express $\frac{38}{16}$ as a mixed number.

   Divide the numerator 38 by the denominator 16.

$$\frac{38}{16} = 2\frac{6}{16}$$

   Express the fractional part $\frac{6}{16}$ in lowest terms.

$$\frac{6 \div 2}{16 \div 2} = \frac{3}{8}$$

   Combine the whole number and fraction.

$$\frac{38}{16} = 2\frac{3}{8}$$

- *Expressing mixed numbers as fractions.* To express a mixed number as a fraction, multiply the whole number by the denominator of the fractional part. Add the numerator of the fractional part. The sum is the numerator of the fraction. The denominator is the same as the denominator of the original fractional part.

Example Express $7\frac{3}{4}$ as a fraction.

Multiply the whole number 7 by the denominator 4 of the fractional part ($7 \times 4 = 28$). Add the numerator 3 of the fractional part to 28. The sum 31 is the numerator of the fraction. The denominator 4 is the same as the denominator of the original fractional part.

$$\frac{7 \times 4 + 3}{4} = \frac{31}{4}$$

or

$$\frac{7}{1} \times \frac{4}{4} = \frac{28}{4}$$

$$\frac{28}{4} + \frac{3}{4} = \frac{31}{4}$$

ADDING FRACTIONS

- Fractions must have a common denominator in order to be added.

- To add fractions, express the fractions as equivalent fractions having the lowest common denominator. Add the numerators and write their sum over the lowest common denominator. Express the fraction in lowest terms.

Example Add: $\frac{3}{8} + \frac{1}{4} + \frac{3}{16} + \frac{1}{32}$

Express the fractions as equivalent fractions with 32 as the denominator.

Add the numerators.

$$\frac{3}{8} = \frac{3}{8} \times \frac{4}{4} = \frac{12}{32}$$

$$\frac{1}{4} = \frac{1}{4} \times \frac{8}{8} = \frac{8}{32}$$

$$\frac{3}{16} = \frac{3}{16} \times \frac{2}{2} = \frac{6}{32}$$

$$+\frac{1}{32} = \qquad \frac{1}{32}$$
$$\frac{27}{32}$$

- After fractions are added, if the numerator is greater than the denominator, the fraction should be expressed as a mixed number.

Example Add: $\frac{1}{2} + \frac{3}{4} + \frac{15}{16} + \frac{11}{16}$

Express the fractions as equivalent fractions with 16 as the denominator.

Add the numerators.

$$\frac{1}{2} = \frac{1}{2} \times \frac{8}{8} = \frac{8}{16}$$

$$\frac{3}{4} = \frac{3}{4} \times \frac{4}{4} = \frac{12}{16}$$

$$\frac{15}{16} = \qquad \frac{15}{16}$$

$$+\frac{11}{16} = \qquad \frac{11}{16}$$
$$\frac{46}{16}$$

Express $\frac{46}{16}$ as a mixed number in lowest terms.

$$\frac{46}{16} = 2\frac{14}{16} = 2\frac{7}{8}$$

ADDING COMBINATIONS OF FRACTIONS, MIXED NUMBERS, AND WHOLE NUMBERS

- To add mixed numbers or combinations of fractions, mixed numbers, and whole numbers, express the fractional parts of the numbers as equivalent fractions having the lowest common denominator. Add the whole numbers. Add the fractions. Combine the whole number and the fraction and express in lowest terms.

Example 1 Add: $3\frac{7}{8} + 5\frac{1}{2} + 9\frac{3}{16}$

Express the fractional parts as equivalent fractions with 16 as the common denominator. Add the whole numbers. Add the fractions. Combine the whole number and the fraction. Express the answer in lowest terms.

$$3\frac{7}{8} = 3\frac{14}{16}$$

$$5\frac{1}{2} = 5\frac{8}{16}$$

$$+9\frac{3}{16} = 9\frac{3}{16}$$

$$17\frac{25}{16} = 17 + 1\frac{9}{16}$$

$$= 18\frac{9}{16}$$

Example 2 Add: $6\frac{3}{4} + \frac{9}{16} + 7\frac{21}{32} + 15$

Express the fractional parts as equivalent fractions with 32 as the common denominator. Add the whole numbers. Add the fractions. Combine the whole number and the fraction. Express the answer in lowest terms.

$$6\frac{3}{4} = 6\frac{24}{32}$$

$$\frac{9}{16} = \frac{18}{32}$$

$$7\frac{21}{32} = 7\frac{21}{32}$$

$$+15 = 15$$

$$28\frac{63}{32} = 28 + 1\frac{31}{32}$$

$$= 29\frac{31}{32}$$

SUBTRACTING FRACTIONS FROM FRACTIONS

- Fractions must have a common denominator in order to be subtracted.

- To subtract a fraction from a fraction, express the fractions as equivalent fractions having the lowest common denominator. Subtract the numerators. Write their difference over the common denominator.

Example Subtract $\frac{3}{4}$ from $\frac{15}{16}$

Express the fractions as equivalent fractions with 16 as the common denominator. Subtract the numerator 12 from the numerator 15. Write the difference 3 over the common denominator 16.

$$\frac{15}{16} = \frac{15}{16}$$

$$-\frac{3}{4} = -\frac{12}{16}$$

$$\frac{3}{16}$$

SUBTRACTING FRACTIONS AND MIXED NUMBERS FROM WHOLE NUMBERS

- To subtract a fraction or a mixed number from a whole number, express the whole number as an equivalent mixed number. The fraction of the mixed number has the same denominator as the denominator of the fraction which is subtracted. Subtract the numerators of the fractions and write their difference over the common denominator. Subtract the whole numbers. Combine the whole number and fraction. Express the answer in lowest terms.

Example 1 Subtract $\frac{3}{8}$ from 7

Express the whole number as an equivalent mixed number with the same denominator as the denominator of the fraction which is subtracted.

Subtract $\dfrac{3}{8}$ from $\dfrac{8}{8}$

Combine whole number and fraction.

$$7 = 6\dfrac{8}{8}$$

$$-\dfrac{3}{8} = -\dfrac{3}{8}$$

$$\overline{\qquad 6\dfrac{5}{8}}$$

Example 2 Subtract $5\dfrac{15}{32}$ from 12

Express the whole number as an equivalent mixed number with the same denominator as the denominator of the fraction which is subtracted.

Subtract fractions.

Subtract whole numbers.

Combine whole number and fraction.

$$12 = 11\dfrac{32}{32}$$

$$- 5\dfrac{15}{32} = - 5\dfrac{15}{32}$$

$$\overline{\qquad 6\dfrac{17}{32}}$$

SUBTRACTING FRACTIONS AND MIXED NUMBERS FROM MIXED NUMBERS

- To subtract a fraction or a mixed number from a mixed number, the fractional part of each number must have the same denominator. Express fractions as equivalent fractions having a common denominator. When the fraction subtracted is larger than the fraction from which it is subtracted, one unit of the whole number is expressed as a fraction with the common denominator. Combine the whole number and fractions. Subtract fractions and subtract whole numbers.

Example 1 Subtract $\dfrac{7}{8}$ from $4\dfrac{3}{16}$

Express the fractions as equivalent fractions with the common denominator 16. Since 14 is larger than 3, express one unit of $4\dfrac{3}{16}$ as a fraction and combine whole number and fractions.

Subtract.

$$4\dfrac{13}{16} = 4\dfrac{3}{16} = 3\dfrac{19}{16}$$

$$- \dfrac{7}{8} = \dfrac{14}{16} = -\dfrac{14}{16}$$

$$\overline{\qquad 3\dfrac{5}{16}}$$

Example 2 Subtract $13\dfrac{1}{4}$ from $20\dfrac{15}{32}$

Express the fractions as equivalent fractions with the common denominator 32.

Subtract fractions.

Subtract whole numbers.

$$20\dfrac{15}{32} = 20\dfrac{15}{32}$$

$$- 13\dfrac{1}{4} = - 13\dfrac{8}{32}$$

$$\overline{\qquad 7\dfrac{7}{32}}$$

MULTIPLYING FRACTIONS

- To multiply two or more fractions, multiply the numerators. Multiply the denominators. Write as a fraction with the product of the numerators over the product of the denominators. Express the answer in lowest terms.

Example 1 Multiply $\dfrac{3}{4} \times \dfrac{5}{8}$

Multiply the numerators.

Multiply the denominators.

Write as a fraction.

$$\frac{3}{4} \times \frac{5}{8} = \frac{15}{32}$$

Example 2 Multiply $\frac{1}{2} \times \frac{2}{3} \times \frac{4}{5}$

Multiply the numerators.

Multiply the denominators.

Write as a fraction and express answer in lowest terms.

$$\frac{1}{2} \times \frac{2}{3} \times \frac{4}{5} = \frac{8}{30} = \frac{4}{15}$$

MULTIPLYING ANY COMBINATION OF FRACTIONS, MIXED NUMBERS, AND WHOLE NUMBERS

- To multiply any combination of fractions, mixed numbers, and whole numbers, write the mixed numbers as fractions. Write whole numbers over the denominator 1. Multiply numerators. Multiply denominators. Express the answer in lowest terms.

Example 1 Multiply $3\frac{1}{4} \times \frac{3}{8}$

Write the mixed number $3\frac{1}{4}$ as the fraction $\frac{13}{4}$.

Multiply the numerators.

Multiply the denominators.

Express as a mixed number.

$$3\frac{1}{4} \times \frac{3}{8} = \frac{13}{4} \times \frac{3}{8} = \frac{39}{32} = 1\frac{7}{32}$$

Example 2 Multiply $2\frac{1}{3} \times 4 \times \frac{4}{5}$

Write the mixed number $2\frac{1}{3}$ as the fraction $\frac{7}{3}$.

Write the whole number 4 over 1.

Multiply the numerators.

Multiply the denominators.

Express as a mixed number.

$$2\frac{1}{3} \times 4 \times \frac{4}{5} = \frac{7}{3} \times \frac{4}{1} \times \frac{4}{5} = \frac{112}{15}$$

$$\frac{112}{15} = 7\frac{7}{15}$$

DIVIDING FRACTIONS

- Division is the inverse of multiplication. Dividing by 4 is the same as multiplying by $\frac{1}{4}$. Four is the inverse of $\frac{1}{4}$ and $\frac{1}{4}$ is the inverse of 4. The inverse of $\frac{5}{16}$ is $\frac{16}{5}$.

- To divide fractions, invert the divisor, change to the inverse operation and multiply. Express the answer in lowest terms.

Example Divide: $\frac{7}{8} \div \frac{2}{3}$

Invert the divisor $\frac{2}{3}$

$\frac{2}{3}$ inverted is $\frac{3}{2}$.

Change to the inverse operation and multiply.

Express as a mixed number.

$$\frac{7}{8} \div \frac{2}{3} = \frac{7}{8} \times \frac{3}{2} = \frac{21}{16} = 1\frac{5}{16}$$

DIVIDING ANY COMBINATION OF FRACTIONS, MIXED NUMBERS, AND WHOLE NUMBERS

- To divide any combination of fractions, mixed numbers, and whole numbers, write the mixed numbers as fractions. Write whole numbers over the denominator 1. Invert the divisor. Change to the inverse operation and multiply. Express the answer in lowest terms.

Example 1 Divide: $6 \div \dfrac{7}{10}$

Write the whole number 6 over the denominator 1.

Invert the divisor $\dfrac{7}{10}$; $\dfrac{7}{10}$ inverted is $\dfrac{10}{7}$.

Change to the inverse operation and multiply.

Express as a mixed number.

$$\frac{6}{1} \div \frac{7}{10} = \frac{6}{1} \times \frac{10}{7} = \frac{60}{7} = 8\frac{4}{7}$$

Example 2 Divide: $\dfrac{3}{4} \div 2\dfrac{1}{5}$

Write the mixed number divisor $2\dfrac{1}{5}$ as the fraction $\dfrac{11}{5}$.

Invert the divisor $\dfrac{11}{5}$; $\dfrac{11}{5}$ inverted is $\dfrac{5}{11}$.

Change to the inverse operation and multiply.

$$\frac{3}{4} \div \frac{11}{5} = \frac{3}{4} \times \frac{5}{11} = \frac{15}{44}$$

Example 3 Divide: $4\dfrac{5}{8} \div 7$

Write the mixed number $4\dfrac{5}{8}$ as the fraction $\dfrac{37}{8}$.

Write the whole number divisor 7 over the denominator 1.

Invert the divisor $\dfrac{7}{1}$; $\dfrac{7}{1}$ inverted is $\dfrac{1}{7}$.

Change to the inverse operation and multiply.

$$\frac{37}{8} \div \frac{7}{1} = \frac{37}{8} \times \frac{1}{7} = \frac{37}{56}$$

ASSIGNMENT

A.   Fractions
Perform the operations indicated.

1. $\dfrac{1}{8} + \dfrac{1}{2} =$ _____ $\dfrac{5}{8}$

2. $\dfrac{3}{16} + \dfrac{1}{4} + \dfrac{7}{8} =$ _____ $\dfrac{21}{16} = 1\dfrac{5}{16}$

3. $\dfrac{3}{4} - \dfrac{1}{2} =$ _____ $\dfrac{1}{4}$

4. $\dfrac{7}{8} - \dfrac{3}{16} =$ _____ $\dfrac{11}{16}$

5. $\dfrac{1}{2} \times \dfrac{1}{4} =$ _____ $\dfrac{1}{8}$

6. $\dfrac{5}{8} \times \dfrac{11}{16} =$ _____ $\dfrac{55}{128}$

7. $\dfrac{3}{4} \div \dfrac{3}{8} =$ _____ $\dfrac{24}{4} = 6$

8. $\dfrac{5}{16} \div \dfrac{3}{8} =$ _____ $\dfrac{40}{48}$

9. $\dfrac{1}{2} + \dfrac{5}{8} - \dfrac{7}{16} =$ _____ $\dfrac{11}{16}$

10. $\dfrac{13}{16} - \dfrac{1}{2} + \dfrac{1}{4} =$ _____ $\dfrac{9}{16}$

B. Mixed Numbers

Perform the operations indicated.

11. $2\frac{14}{4} + 6\frac{5}{16} = $ __$8\frac{9}{16}$__

12. $9\frac{5}{8} + 3\frac{3}{4} = $ __$13\frac{3}{8}$__

13. $7\frac{1}{2} + 2\frac{21}{32} = $ __$9\frac{37}{32} = 10\frac{5}{32}$__ ✓

14. $8\frac{1}{4} - 1\frac{1}{16} = $ __$7\frac{3}{16}$__ ✓

15. $13\frac{5}{8} - 3\frac{5}{16} = $ __$10\frac{5}{16}$__ ✓

16. $11\frac{1}{4} - 8\frac{5}{8} = $ __$-3\frac{3}{8}$__

17. $1\frac{1}{2} \times 8\frac{1}{4} = $ __$8\frac{1}{8}$__ $\frac{3}{2}\frac{33}{4}$ $\frac{99}{8}$

18. $3\frac{5}{8} \times 2\frac{1}{16} = $ __$6\frac{5}{128}$__ $12\frac{3}{8}$

19. $2\frac{1}{4} \div 1\frac{1}{4} = $ __$\frac{36}{20}$__ $1\frac{16}{20} = 1\frac{4}{5}$

20. $\frac{5}{8} \div 3\frac{3}{16} = $ _____ $\frac{5}{8} \times \frac{51}{16}$ $\frac{255}{128} = 1\frac{127}{128}$

UNIT 10   Decimals

OBJECTIVES

After completing this unit, you will be able to:

- round off decimal fractions.
- add, subtract, multiply, and divide decimal fractions.
- convert between decimal fractions and common fractions.

ROUNDING DECIMAL FRACTIONS

- To round a decimal fraction, locate the digit in the number that gives the desired number of decimal places. Increase that digit by 1 if the digit that directly follows is 5 or more. Do not change the value of the digit if the digit which follows is less than 5. Drop all digits that follow.

    Example 1   Round 0.63861 to 3 decimal places.

    Locate the digit in the third place (8). The fourth decimal-place digit, 6, is greater than 5 and increases the third decimal-place digit 8, to 9. Drop all digits that follow.

    $$0.63\underline{8}61 \approx 0.639$$

Example 2   Round 3.0746 to 2 decimal places.

Locate the digit in the second decimal place (7). The third decimal-place digit 4 is less than 5 and does not change the value of the second decimal-place digit 7. Drop all digits which follow.

$$3.0\underline{7}46 \approx 3.07$$

ADDING DECIMAL FRACTIONS

- To add decimal fractions, arrange the numbers so that the decimal points are directly under each other. The decimal point of a whole number is directly to the right of the last digit. Add each column as with whole numbers. Place the decimal point in the sum directly under the other decimal points.

Example Add: 7.65 + 208.062 + 0.009 + 36 + 5.1037

> Arrange the numbers so that the decimal points are directly under each other.
>
> Add zeros so that all numbers have the same number of places to the right of the decimal point.
>
> Add each column of numbers.
>
> Place the decimal point in the sum directly under the other decimal points.

$$\begin{array}{r} 7.6500 \\ 208.0620 \\ 0.0090 \\ 36.0000 \\ +\quad 5.1037 \\ \hline 256.8247 \end{array}$$

SUBTRACTING DECIMAL FRACTIONS

- To subtract decimal fractions, arrange the numbers so that the decimal points are directly under each other. Subtract each column as with whole numbers. Place the decimal point in the difference directly under the other decimal points.

Example Subtract: 87.4 − 42.125

> Arrange the numbers so that the decimal points are directly under each other. Add zeros so that the numbers have the same number of places to the right of the decimal point.
>
> Subtract each column of numbers.
>
> Place the decimal point in the difference directly under the other decimal points.

$$\begin{array}{r} 87.400 \\ -\ 42.125 \\ \hline 45.275 \end{array}$$

MULTIPLYING DECIMAL FRACTIONS

- To multiply decimal fractions, multiply using the same procedure as with whole numbers. Count the number of decimal places in both the multiplier and the multiplicand. Begin counting from the last digit on the right of the product and place the decimal point the same number of places as there are in both the multiplicand and the multiplier.

Example Multiply: 50.216 × 1.73

> Multiply as with whole numbers.
>
> Count the number of decimal places in the multiplier (2 places) and the multiplicand (3 places).
>
> Beginning at the right of the product, place the decimal point the same number of places as there are in both the multiplicand and the multiplier (5 places).

$$\begin{array}{r} 50.216 \quad \text{Multiplicand (3 places)} \\ \times\quad 1.73 \quad \text{Multiplier (2 places)} \\ \hline 150648 \\ 351512 \\ 50216 \quad \text{(5 places)} \\ \hline 86.87368 \end{array}$$

- When multiplying certain decimal fractions, the product has a smaller number of digits than the number of decimal places required. For these products, add as many zeros to the left of the product as are necessary to give the required number of decimal places.

Example Multiply: 0.27 × 0.18

> Multiply as with whole numbers.

The product must have 4 decimal places.

Add one zero to the left of the product.

$$
\begin{array}{r}
0.27 \quad \text{(2 places)} \\
\times\ 0.18 \quad \text{(2 places)} \\
\hline
216 \\
27 \\
\hline
0.0486 \quad \text{(4 places)}
\end{array}
$$

DIVIDING DECIMAL FRACTIONS

- To divide decimal fractions, use the same procedure as with whole numbers. Move the decimal point of the divisor as many places to the right as necessary to make the divisor a whole number. Move the decimal point of the dividend the same number of places to the right. Add zeros to the dividend if necessary. Place the decimal point in the answer directly above the decimal point in the dividend. Divide as with whole numbers. Zeros may be added to the dividend to give the number of decimal places required in the answer.

    Example 1 Divide: $0.6150 \div 0.75$

    Move the decimal point 2 places to the right in the divisor.

    Move the decimal point 2 places in the dividend.

    Place the decimal point in the answer directly above the decimal point in the dividend.

    Divide as with whole numbers.

$$
\text{Divisor} \longrightarrow 0.75 \overline{)\ 0\ 61.50} \longleftarrow \text{Dividend}
$$
$$
\begin{array}{r}
0.82 \\
\hline
60\ 0 \\
\hline
1\ 50 \\
1\ 50
\end{array}
$$

Example 2 Divide: $10.7 \div 4.375$. Round the answer to 3 decimal places.

Move the decimal point 3 places to the right in the divisor.

Move the decimal point 3 places in the dividend, adding 2 zeros.

Place the decimal point in the answer directly above the decimal point in the dividend.

Add 4 zeros to the dividend. One more zero is added than the number of decimal places required in the answer.

Divide as with whole numbers.

$$
\begin{array}{r}
2.4457 \quad \approx 2.446 \\
4\,375.\overline{)10\,700.0000} \\
\underline{8\ 750} \\
1\ 950\ 0 \\
\underline{1\ 750\ 0} \\
200\ 00 \\
\underline{175\ 00} \\
25\ 000 \\
\underline{21\ 875} \\
3\ 1250 \\
\underline{3\ 0625} \\
625
\end{array}
$$

EXPRESSING COMMON FRACTIONS AS DECIMAL FRACTIONS

- A common fraction is an indicated division. A common fraction is expressed as a decimal fraction by dividing the numerator by the denominator.

    Example Express $\frac{5}{8}$ as a decimal fraction.

    Write $\frac{5}{8}$ as an indicated division.

$$
8 \overline{)5}
$$

Place a decimal point after the 5 and add zeros to the right of the decimal point.

$$8 \overline{)\ 5.000}$$

Place the decimal point for the answer directly above the decimal point in the dividend.

$$8 \overline{)\ 5.000}^{\ .}$$

Divide.

$$8 \overline{)\ 5.000}^{\ 0.625}$$

- A common fraction which will not divide evenly is expressed as a repeating decimal.

Example Express $\frac{1}{3}$ as a decimal.

Write $\frac{1}{3}$ as an indicated division.

Place a decimal point after the 1 and add zeros to the right of the decimal point. Place the decimal point for the answer directly above the decimal point in the dividend.

$$3 \overline{)\ 1.0000}^{\ .}$$

Divide.

$$3 \overline{)\ 1.0000}^{\ 0.3333}$$

ASSIGNMENT

A. Decimal Exercises

Perform the indicated operations and round the answer to 2 places.

1. $7.55 + 2.341 =$ ___9.89___

2. $2.75 + 4.450 + 11.6 =$ ___18.80___

3. $1.58 + 13.9666 + 14.33333 =$ ___29.88___

4. $2.87 - 1.04 =$ ___1.83___

5. $8.754 - 2.227 =$ ___6.53___

EXPRESSING DECIMAL FRACTIONS AS COMMON FRACTIONS

- To express a decimal fraction as a common fraction, write the number after the decimal point as the numerator of a common fraction. Write the denominator as 1 followed by as many zeros as there are digits to the right of the decimal point. Express the common fraction in lowest terms.

Example 1 Express 0.9 as a common fraction.

Write 9 as the numerator.

Write the denominator as 1 followed by 1 zero. The denominator is 10.

$$\frac{9}{10}$$

Example 2 Express 0.125 as a common fraction.

Write 125 as the numerator.

Write the denominator as 1 followed by 3 zeros. The denominator is 1000.

$$\frac{125}{1000}$$

Express the fraction in lowest terms.

$$\frac{125}{1000} = \frac{1}{8}$$

6. 6.53 – 3.875 = __2.66__ ✓

7. 2.8 × 1.5 = __4.20__ ✓

8. 0.85 × 0.3333 = __.28__ ✓

9. 1.5 × 0.2375 = __0.36__ ✓

10. 0.625 ÷ 3 = __.21__ ✓

11. 1.13 ÷ 2.4884 = __.45__ ✓

12. 14.75 ÷ 4.25 = __3.47__ ✓

B. Converting Common Fractions to Decimal Fractions
Convert the following to decimals:

13. $\frac{3}{4}$ = __.75__ ✓

14. $\frac{13}{16}$ = __.81__ ✓

15. $3\frac{5}{8}$ = __3.625__ ✓

16. $9\frac{15}{16}$ = __9.9375__

17. $2\frac{9}{32}$ = __2.28125__

C. Converting Decimals to Common Fractions
Convert the following to common fractions:

18. 0.875 = __7/8__ ✓

19. 1.75 = __1 3/4__ ✓

20. 4.625 = __4 5/8__ ✓

21. 0.375 = __3/8__ ✓

22. 8.8125 = __8 13/16__ ✓

UNIT 11 Measurement and Area

OBJECTIVES

After completing this unit, you will be able to:

- convert feet, inches, and common fractions of inches to decimals.
- convert feet and decimal fractions of feet to feet and inches.
- compute the area of rectangles, triangles, and circles.
- find the length of the unknown side of a right triangle when the other two sides are known.

EXPRESSING INCHES AS FEET AND INCHES

- There are 12 inches in 1 foot.
- To express inches as feet and inches, divide the given length in inches by 12 to obtain the number of whole feet. The remainder is the number of inches in addition to the number of whole feet. The answer is the number of whole feet plus the remainder in inches.

  Example 1 Express $176 \frac{7}{16}$ inches as feet and inches.

Divide $176 \frac{7}{16}$ inches by 12.

There are 14 feet plus a remainder of $8 \frac{7}{16}$ inches.

$$
\begin{array}{r}
14 \ (\text{feet}) \\
12 \overline{)\ 176 \ \frac{7}{16}} \\
\underline{12} \\
56 \\
\underline{48} \\
8 \ \frac{7}{16} \leftarrow \text{Remainder (inches)}
\end{array}
$$

$$14' - 8 \frac{7''}{16}$$

Example 2   Express 54.2 inches as feet and inches.

Divide 54.2 inches by 12.

There are 4 feet plus a remainder of 6.2 inches.

$$
\begin{array}{r}
4 \text{ (feet)} \\
12 \overline{)\ 54.2} \\
\underline{48} \\
6.2 \leftarrow \text{Remainder} \\
\text{(inches)}
\end{array}
$$

4 feet 6.2 inches.

EXPRESSING FEET AND INCHES AS INCHES

- There are 12 inches in one foot.
- To express feet and inches as inches, multiply the number of feet in the given length by 12. To this product, add the number of inches in the given length.

  Example   Express 7 feet $9\frac{3}{4}$ inches as inches.

    Multiply 7 feet by 12. There are 84 inches in 7 feet.

$$7 \times 12 = 84$$

Add $9\frac{3}{4}$ inches to 84 inches.

$$84 \text{ inches} + 9\frac{3}{4} \text{ inches} = 93\frac{3}{4} \text{ inches}$$

EXPRESSING INCHES AS DECIMAL FRACTIONS OF A FOOT

- An inch is $\frac{1}{12}$ of a foot. To express whole inches as a decimal part of a foot, divide the number of inches by 12.

  Example   Express 7 inches as a decimal fraction of a foot.

    Divide 7 by 12.

$$7 \div 12 = 0.58$$

- To express a common fraction of an inch as a decimal fraction of a foot, express the common fraction as a decimal, then divide the decimal by 12.

  Example 1   Express $\frac{3}{4}$ inch as a decimal fraction of a foot.

    Express $\frac{3}{4}$ as a decimal.

$$3 \div 4 = 0.75$$

Divide the decimal by 12.

$$0.75 \div 12 = 0.06$$

0.06 feet

Example 2   Express $4\frac{3}{4}$ inches as a decimal fraction of a foot.

Express $4\frac{3}{4}$ as a decimal.

$$4 + \frac{3}{4} = 4 + 0.75 = 4.75$$

Divide the decimal inches by 12.

$$4.75 \div 12 = 0.39$$

0.39 feet

EXPRESSING DECIMAL FRACTIONS OF A FOOT AS INCHES

- To express a decimal part of a foot as decimal inches multiply by 12.

  Example   Express 0.62 feet as inches.

    Multiply 0.62 by 12.

$$0.62 \times 12 = 7.44$$

7.44 inches

AREA MEASURE

- A surface is measured by determining the number of surface units contained in it. A surface is two dimensional. It has length and width, but no thickness. Both length and width must be expressed in the same unit of measure. Area is expressed in square units. For example, 5 feet X 8 feet equals 40 square feet.

- *Equivalent Units of Area Measure:*

    1 square foot (sq ft) =
    12 inches X 12 inches = 144 square inches (sq in)

    1 square yard (sq yd) =
    3 feet X 3 feet = 9 square feet (sq ft)

- To express a given unit of area as a larger unit of area, divide the given area by the number of square units contained in one of the larger units.

    Example 1 Express 648 square inches as square feet.

    Since 144 sq in = 1 sq ft, divide 648 by 144.

    648 ÷ 144 = 4.5
    648 square inches = 4.5 square feet

    Example 2 Express 28.8 square feet as square yards.

    Since 9 sq ft = 1 sq yd, divide 28.8 by 9.

    28.8 ÷ 9 = 3.2
    28.8 square feet = 3.2 square yards

- To express a given unit of area as a smaller unit of area, multiply the given area by the number of square units contained in one of the larger units.

    Example 1 Express 7.5 square feet as square inches.

    Since 144 sq in = 1 sq ft, multiply 7.5 by 144.

    7.5 X 144 = 1080
    7.5 square feet = 1080 square inches

Example 2 Express 23 square yards as square feet.

Since 9 sq ft = 1 sq yd, multiply 23 by 9.

23 X 9 = 207
23 square yards = 207 square feet

- *Computing Areas of Common Geometric Figures:*

    Rectangle A rectangle is a four-sided plane figure with 4 right (90°) angles.

    The area of a rectangle is equal to the product of its length and its width.

    Area = length X width (A = 1 X w)

    Example Find the area of a rectangle 24 feet long and 13 feet wide.

    A = 1 X w

    A = 24 ft X 13 ft

    A = 312 square feet

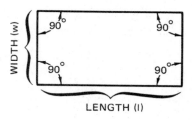

    Triangle A triangle is a plane figure with 3 sides and 3 angles.

    The area of a triangle is equal to one-half the product of its base and altitude.

    $$A = \frac{1}{2} \text{ base} \times \text{altitude} \quad (A = \frac{1}{2} b \times a)$$

    Example Find the area of a triangle with a base of 16 feet and an altitude of 12 feet.

$$A = \frac{1}{2} b \times a$$

$$A = \frac{1}{2} \times 16 \text{ ft} \times 12 \text{ ft}$$

$$A = 96 \text{ square feet}$$

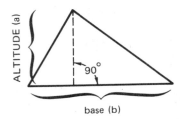

Circle The area of a circle is equal to π times the square of its radius.

Area $= \pi \times$ radius^2 $(A = \pi \times r^2)$

Note: π (pronounced "pi") is approximately equal to 3.14. Radius squared (r^2) means $r \times r$.

Example Find the area of a circle with a 15-inch radius.

$A = \pi \times r^2$

$A = 3.14 \times (15 \text{ in})^2$

$A = 3.14 \times 225 \text{ sq in}$

$A = 706.5 \text{ square inches}$

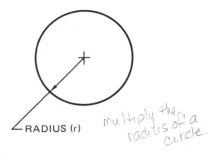

RADIUS (r)   *multiply the radius of a circle.*

FINDING AN UNKNOWN SIDE OF A RIGHT TRIANGLE, GIVEN TWO SIDES

- If one of the angles of a triangle is a right (90°) angle, the figure is called a right triangle. The side opposite the right angle is called the hypotenuse. In the figure shown, c is opposite the right angle; c is the hypotenuse.

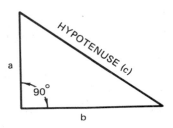

- In a right triangle, the square of the hypotenuse is equal to the sum of the squares of the other two sides:

$$c^2 = a^2 + b^2$$

If any two sides of a right triangle are known, the length of the third side can be determined by one of the following formulas:

$$c^2 = \sqrt{a^2 + b^2}$$

$$a^2 = \sqrt{c^2 - b^2}$$

$$b^2 = \sqrt{c^2 - a^2}$$

Example In the right triangle shown, a = 6 ft, b = 8 ft, find c.

$$c = \sqrt{a^2 + b^2}$$

$$c = \sqrt{6^2 + 8^2}$$

$$c = \sqrt{36 + 64}$$

$$c = \sqrt{100}$$

$$c = \quad 10 \text{ feet}$$

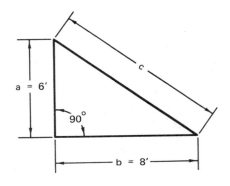

Example In the right triangle shown, c = 30 ft, b = 20 ft, find a.

$$a = \sqrt{c^2 - b^2}$$

$$a = \sqrt{30^2 - 20^2}$$

$$a = \sqrt{900 - 400}$$

$$a = \sqrt{500}$$

$$a = \quad 22.36 \text{ feet (to 2 decimal places)}$$

Example In the right triangle shown, c = 18 ft, a = 6 ft, find b.

$$b = \sqrt{c^2 - a^2}$$

$$b = \sqrt{18^2 - 6^2}$$

$$b = \sqrt{324 - 36}$$

$$b = \sqrt{288}$$

$$b = \quad 16.97 \text{ feet (to 2 decimal places)}$$

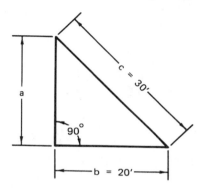

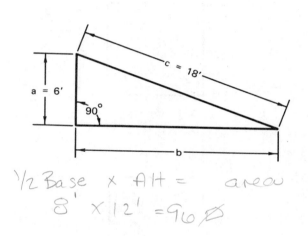

½ Base × Alt = area
8' × 12' = 96 Ø

ASSIGNMENT

A.   Converting Feet and Inches

Express the following as feet and decimal fractions of a foot.

1. 5'-6" = _5½_   5.5 ✓

2. 18'-9" = _18 3/4_   18.75

3. 4'-7" = _4 7/12_   4.583

4. 9'-6½" = _9 13/24_   9.5416

5. 15'-11¾" = _15 45/48_   15.9375

6. 39⅝" = _3.3020833._

7. 12¾" = _1.075_   0625

8. 104 7/16" = _8._

9. 119 15/16" = ____

10. 9 3/32" = ____

12 inches = 1 ft
144 sq in = 1 sq ft
12×12=144   9 sq ft = 1 sq yard
☐×3 = 9   27 cubic feet = 1 cubic yard

B.   Area

Compute the area in square inches and decimal fractions of square inches. Round the results to 2 places.

11.

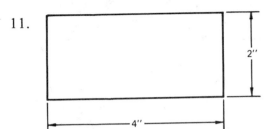

_8_
____

12.

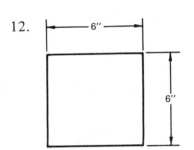

_36_

13.

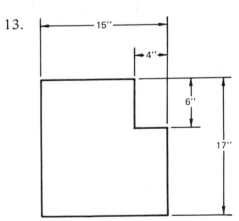

255 - 24 = 231

_231_

14.

20"

18"

_180_

½ base × Alt = area

Base × ½ Alt = area

18 × 10   = 180 sq In

½ base × Alt = Area
19.75 × 9.625 = 190.09

15.

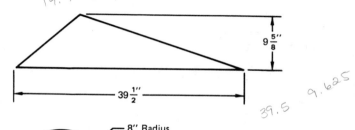

$9\frac{5}{8}''$

$39\frac{1}{2}''$

39.5   9.625

190.09

16.

8" Radius

3.14 × 8 = 25.12

25.12

17.

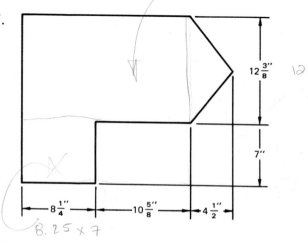

$12\frac{3}{8}''$ 12.375 × .875

7"

$8\frac{1}{4}''$ $10\frac{5}{8}''$ $4\frac{1}{2}''$

8.25 × 7

319.17 ▱

C.   Triangles
Find the length of the unknown side.

18.

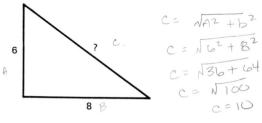

6

A

?   c.

8   B

$c = \sqrt{A^2 + b^2}$

$c = \sqrt{6^2 + 8^2}$

$c = \sqrt{36 + 64}$

$c = \sqrt{100}$

$c = 10$

10

19.

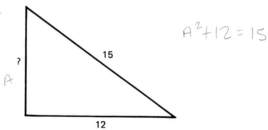

?

A

15

12

$A^2 + 12 = 15$

9

20.

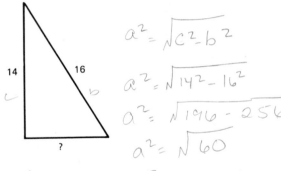

$$a^2 = \sqrt{c^2 - b^2}$$

$$a^2 = \sqrt{14^2 - 16^2}$$

$$a^2 = \sqrt{196 - 256}$$

$$a^2 = \sqrt{60}$$

$$a^2 = 7.75$$

<u>7.75</u>

21.

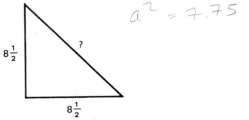

_____

22.

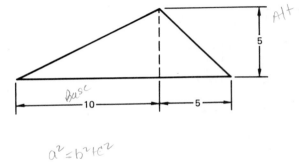

$$a^2 = b^2 + c^2$$

_____

Section 3
Trade Sketching

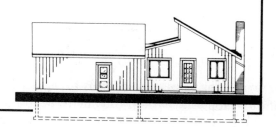

UNIT 12   Sketching Straight Lines

OBJECTIVES

After completing this unit, you will be able to:

- sketch straight lines.
- explain proportion in sketching.

IMPORTANCE OF SKETCHING

The old saying "a picture is worth a thousand words," is particularly true to construction workers. To them a drawing is a set of instructions. They read drawings as others would read a manual of instructions. The engineer, architect, or foreman uses a pencil sketch to illustrate an idea.

A worker on the job who thinks of a time-saving device or a new method of construction uses a sketch to explain the idea to others. In many cases, a pencil sketch that has been suitably initialed is used as authority to proceed with a job. Even the language barrier offers no handicap to the foreman who has a pencil and paper handy.

The pencil sketch plays an important part in the building trades. Any worker in these trades who wants to become a foreman or superintendent should be able to draw neat sketches.

Sketches are used in many cases instead of instrument drawings because they can be made so quickly and do not require any tools other than paper, pencil, and eraser. In order to be useful, however, the sketch should be carefully and neatly drawn. The lines should be clean and straight. The information contained in the sketch should be complete. Although measuring instruments are not used, the proportions of the object to be sketched should be reasonably accurate.

SKETCHING STRAIGHT LINES

Most of us can draw a short line freehand and it will appear to be straight. Long lines, however, present a difficulty. There are several tricks that can be used to help in

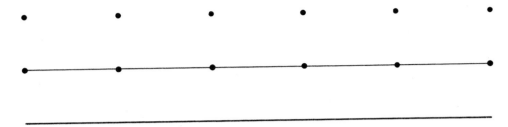

Fig. 12-1 Sketching straight lines

drawing long lines. One trick is to use a series of dots along the path of the line to be drawn.

Instead of sketching the entire line, lay out a row of dots about 1 inch apart, figure 12-1. Now hold the paper up and sight along this row of dots. Any dot that is out of line shows up immediately and can easily be shifted so that all the dots are in line. To draw a light line connecting each of the dots is a relatively simple job. As a final step, go over the entire line with a single stroke, making it the desired weight. With practice, you will be able to increase the distance between dots and, eventually, eliminate them entirely.

Horizontal lines are best drawn from left to right if you are right-handed, figure 12-2. Left-handed sketchers should draw from right to left. These lines should be drawn with a forearm rather than a wrist movement. While pivoting from the wrist may be a somewhat easier movement, it will cause a curve when drawing longer lines. When a series of lines are

to be drawn, it is a good practice to first sketch all lines lightly. When you are sure that your sketch is correct, the lines can all be darkened at the same time. This eliminates much erasing and serves to keep the sketch clean.

Vertical lines are best drawn from the top down, figure 12-3. As in drawing horizontal lines, the forearm should be used as a pivot point. Long, vertical lines can be drawn by using the row of dots as an aid. To draw lines parallel, as they are shown in figure 12-3, use a piece of paper as a ruler to mark off equal distances at each end of a line. A line sketched through these two points will be parallel to the first line.

PROPORTION

Proportion is illustrated in figure 12-4. Assume that the object has the dimensions shown by the solid outline. If one side Ⓐ of

Fig. 12-2 Horizontal lines

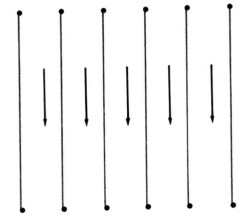

Fig. 12-3 Vertical lines

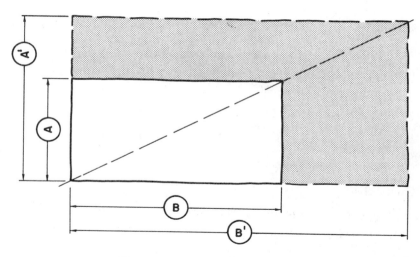

Fig. 12-4 Proportional sketching

this rectangle is drawn to a larger scale, the other side (B) must be lengthened the same proportional amount. If side (B) were lengthened the same amount as side (A), the drawing would no longer be a true picture of the same object.

The correct proportions are extremely important in freehand sketching. Since no measuring tools are used in freehand sketching, it is more difficult to show the accurate shape. The actual sizes used in a sketch are relatively unimportant. A line may be drawn two inches long and dimensioned five inches, but whatever unit of measure is used, the entire sketch must be made to that scale if the proportions are to be correct. Sketching an object freehand is not an excuse for distorting the proportions of the object.

Objects should be sketched in the same position as they appear, figure 12-5. Notes should be neatly lettered so that they can be read from the bottom of the paper. Dimensions are read from the bottom and right side of the drawing.

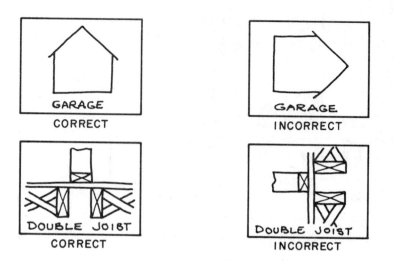

Fig. 12-5 Sketch objects in the proper position

ASSIGNMENT

A.   Sketching

Step 1 Make a three-view freehand sketch of the concrete foundation complete with dimensions.

Step 2 Let each square of the drawing sheet represent 12″.

Step 3 Indicate a break line in the front and right-side views.

B.   Questions

1. What is the overall height of the foundation including the footing? _____

2. What is the width of the footing? _____

3. How thick is the concrete wall? _____

4. How much does the footing project beyond each face of the foundation wall? _____

5. What is the difference in length of the two walls which form the corner? _____

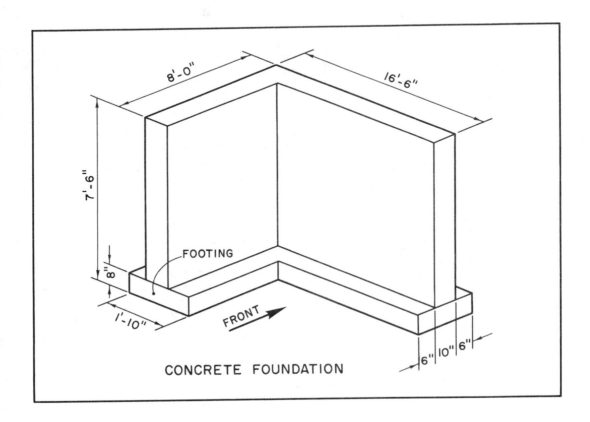

CONCRETE FOUNDATION

ASSIGNMENT UNIT ⑫   DR. BY   CH. BY   RATING

UNIT 13 Sketching Circles, Arcs, and Irregular Shapes

OBJECTIVES

After completing this unit, you will be able to:

- lay out and sketch small and large-diameter circles and arcs.
- lay out and sketch irregular shapes.

CIRCLES AND ARCS

Circles and parts of circles (arcs) are more difficult to sketch than straight lines. To simplify this operation, there are several techniques which can be used.

One of the main causes of poorly sketched circles is the fact that beginners try to draw the entire circle by sight and in one stroke. Like all other drawing details, a circle or an arc should be carefully laid out before it is drawn.

Notice that the circle in figure 13-1 bears some geometric resemblance to a square. Its length and height are the same size as are those of the square. If the square were circumscribed about the circle as shown, it can be seen that the two figures are tangent to each other at four points. These points are

the intersections of the centerlines of the circle and the midpoints of the sides of the square.

Since the square is relatively easy to sketch, it can be used as the beginning point for sketching the circle. The procedure for sketching a circle is as follows:

Step 1 Sketch a square of the same size as the diameter of the required circle.

Step 2 Mark off the midpoint of each of the four sides (A, B, C, and D).

Step 3 Sketch lines A-B and C-D. These lines represent the vertical and horizontal centerlines of the circle. They divide the square into four smaller squares, figure 13-2.

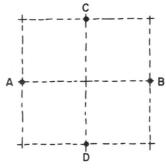

Fig. 13-2

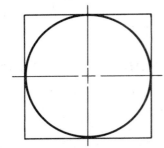

Fig. 13-1 A square circumscribed about a circle

Step 4 In each of the four squares, sketch an arc that is tangent to two sides of the square. Sketch these arcs with light, feathered strokes as shown in figure 13-3.

Step 5 When the four separate arcs have been sketched roughly, make any necessary sketching strokes to blend them completely into one smooth curve.

Step 6 Go over the outline of the circle with a single stroke so that the circle is drawn with the same line weight as the rest of the sketch.

SKETCHING LARGE-DIAMETER CIRCLES OR ARCS

The method outlined above is useful for the beginner in sketching small-diameter circles. Instead of working from a single reference point, the center of the circle, there are four such points to help in sketching a smooth outline. For large-diameter circles, however, four reference points are not enough to produce a smooth curve. The resultant circle, drawn with only four reference points, will usually consist of four flattened-out or otherwise distorted arcs.

The construction of a large-diameter circle requires the use of additional reference points which may be achieved in the following manner:

Step 1 Lay out centerlines A-B and C-D as shown in figure 13-4.

Step 2 Sketch in lines E-F and G-H. These diagonal lines should approximately bisect each of the four right angles which are formed by the two centerlines.

Step 3 Sketch in additional diagonal lines to subdivide all of the angles again as shown. Note: The larger the diameter of the circle, the more diagonal lines will be needed to produce a smoothly curved circle or arc.

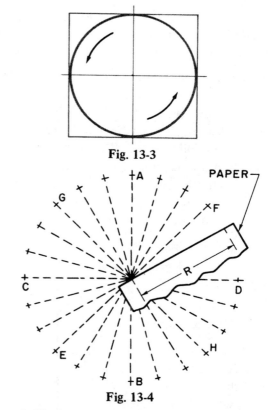

Fig. 13-3

Fig. 13-4

Step 4 Mark off the required radius from the center on each of the diagonal lines. To insure accuracy, the distance should be marked off on the edge of a sheet of paper and then transferred to each of the construction lines of the sketch.

Step 5 Sketch the circle with short strokes so that it passes through each of the reference points. Up to this point, all of the construction lines should be drawn as very light lines so that they will not interfere with the finished outline.

Step 6 Complete the circle with a solid, single-stroke line so that it blends with the rest of the sketch.

SKETCHING AN IRREGULAR SHAPE

Sketching an irregularly shaped object requires the use of many reference points. For such sketches, the use of graph paper, as shown in figure 13-5, greatly simplifies the drawing.

Figure 13-5 shows the steps to follow in sketching an object or a workpiece with a nonuniform or irregular shape.

Step 1   Lay out a series of equally spaced vertical and horizontal lines across the view to be sketched. The space between the lines will depend on the complexity of the shape. For the most accurate reproduction, the lines should be fairly close together. This condition will provide the greatest number of reference points.

Step 2   On a blank sheet of graph paper that has the same size squares as the original, plot each of the reference points as it appears on the original.

Step 3   Sketch in lightly the irregular shape so that it passes through each of the reference points.

Step 4   Darken the outline so that it blends in with the other lines of the sketch.

This method of sketching can also be used to make a sketch to a reduced or an enlarged scale. If the sketch is made on graph paper that has smaller or larger squares than the original layout, the finished sketch will be in perfect proportion to the original but will be either smaller or larger as desired.

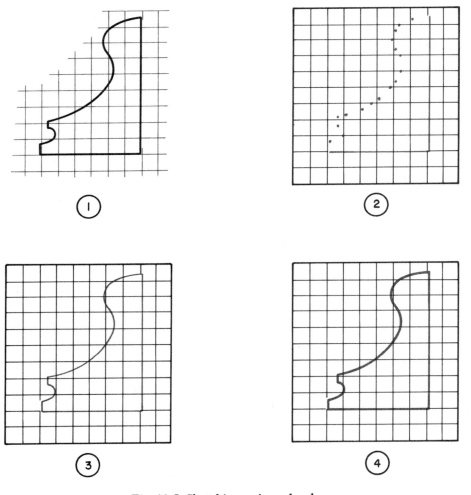

Fig. 13-5 Sketching an irregular shape

ASSIGNMENT

A.   Sketching

Step 1 Make a two-view working sketch of the pipe chair. Make the sketch full size.

Step 2 Show all dimensions and centerlines.

B.   Questions

1. What is the width of the base of the pipe chair?   _____

2. What is the height from the top of the base to the bottom of the 1″ radius?   _____

3. How far does the base project beyond the faces of the vertical members?   _____

4. Which two views will show the complete shape outline and all the necessary dimensions?   _____

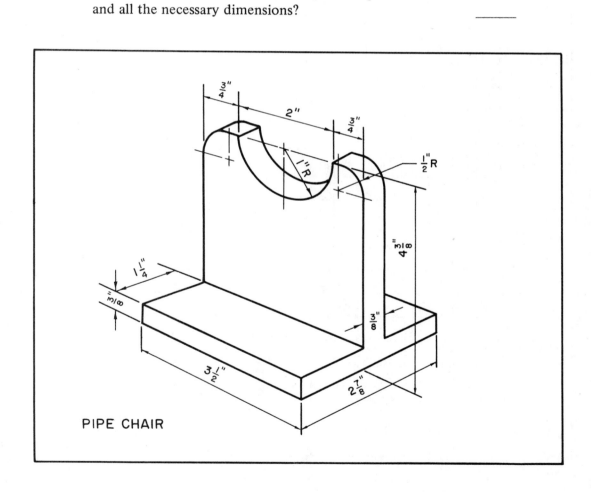

PIPE CHAIR

ASSIGNMENT UNIT ⑬   DR.BY   CH.BY   RATING

UNIT 14 Isometric Sketching

OBJECTIVES

After completing this unit, you will be able to:

- explain the principles of isometric sketching and drawing.
- Sketch rectangular shapes in isometric.

There are many construction details in a typical set of building plans that can best be explained or shown by using a pictoral drawing rather than orthographic projection. Several types of pictoral drawings have been developed for this purpose: isometric, oblique, and perspective drawings.   These types are the most widely used for construction drawings, figure 14-1.

In each of these drawing styles the objective is not a flowery, artistic picture, but rather a drawing that shows shapes, locations, and

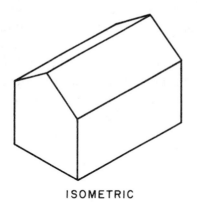

ISOMETRIC

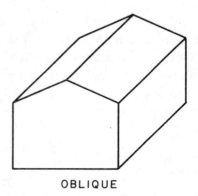

OBLIQUE

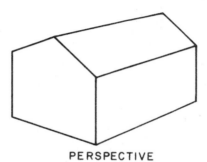

PERSPECTIVE

Fig. 14-1 Common types of pictorial drawings

dimensions of construction details. This must be done in a manner that is readily understandable to the workers who must use the drawings as instructions for the construction work.

The isometric drawing is one of the simplest types of drawings to make. It combines three views of the orthographic projection in a single picture, figure 14-2. By including the dimensions, this single sketch presents a set of instructions which are easy to follow and visualize.

To the construction worker who has an understanding of the orthographic form of trade drawing, the making of an isometric sketch or drawing is relatively simple. There are two basic rules to follow:

- Lines which are vertical in an orthographic elevation remain vertical in the isometric sketch.

- Lines which are horizontal in an orthographic elevation are projected at an angle of 30 degrees in an isometric sketch.

The word *isometric* means equal measure. In its application to drawing, it simply means that straight lines are drawn to their true length regardless of the fact that the views are projected at an angle. This removes the element of guesswork or judgment of the length of lines.

HOW TO MAKE AN ISOMETRIC SKETCH

The isometric sketch is started from three axes: the vertical axis which is common to the front and the end elevations (Line 1), and the two horizontal lines which represent the bottom surface of both of these views (Lines 2 and 3), figures 14-3 and 14-4. To make an isometric sketch of the notched block shown in the illustration, follow steps outlined below.

Step 1   Draw a light, long, vertical line to represent Line 1. Position it on the paper so that there is room for the rest of the sketch. Draw long, light guidelines to represent Lines 2 and 3. Draw these lines, representing the horizontal axes, at an angle of 30 degrees from the horizontal direction. To help estimate a 30-degree angle, remember that it is one-third of a right angle, figure 14-5.

Step 2   Mark off the overall height of the notched block on Line 1, the overall length on Line 2, and the overall width on Line 3 as indicated. Draw light lines through these points to complete the solid, rectangular outline which represents the basic shape of the notched block, figure 14-6.

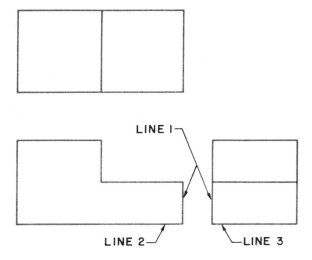

Fig. 14-3   Orthographic lines

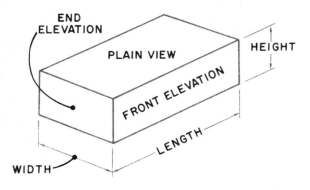

Fig. 14-2   Isometric drawing

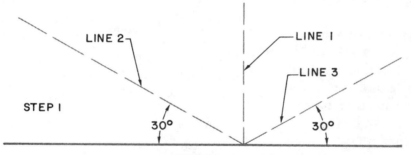

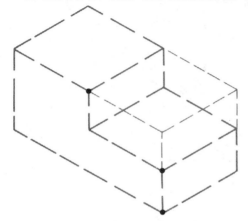

Fig. 14-4 Isometric Axes

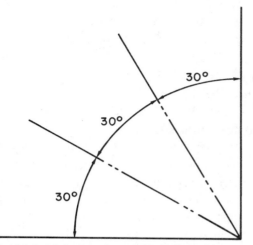

Fig. 14-5 30 degrees is one-third of a right angle

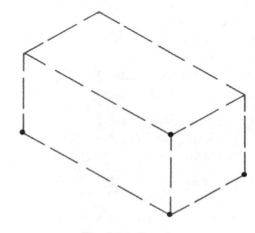

Fig. 14-6 Step 2

Step 3 Mark off the length and height of the notch on the lines of the front elevation. Through these points sketch in the vertical and horizontal lines of the notch. Project the ends of these lines as shown so that the surfaces of the notch appear in all views of the isometric sketch, figure 14-7.

Step 4 Remove all unnecessary guidelines from the sketch and go over the outline with solid, single-stroke object lines, figure 14-8.

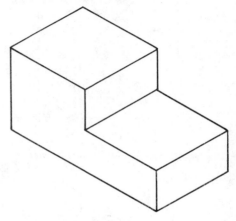

Fig. 14-7 Step 3

Fig. 14-8 Step 4

SKETCHING ANGLES IN ISOMETRIC

Since an isometric drawing is already projected at an angle to the viewer, the layout of any angular lines or surfaces cannot be done with a triangle or a protractor. This is because the drawing is in an orthographic pro-

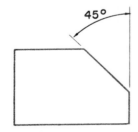

Fig. 14-9 Chamfered block

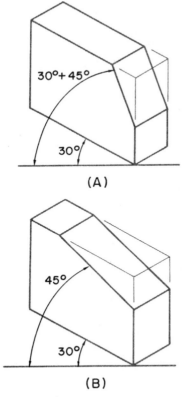

(A)

(B)

Fig. 14-10 Incorrectly drawn isometric

jection. For example, if the 45-degree angle shown in figure 14-9 is drawn isometrically by adding it to the basic 30-degree angle, the result is figure 14-10A.

If the 45-degree angle is measured from the horizontal direction, the result is figure 14-10B. In either case, the projection is a severe distortion of the chamfered block.

The proper method of projecting an angular line in an isometric is to determine the location of each end of the line, mark off these locations on the vertical and horizontal axes, then draw the line through these points. In the illustration there is a 45-degree angle on each end of the wood block. Note that in figure 14-11, the extremities of each of these lines have been marked off on the vertical and horizontal lines.

Remember that it is only the vertical and horizontal lines of a drawing that are drawn to their true length in an isometric. Angular lines are drawn either longer or shorter than in a flat view, depending on which side of the workpiece they are located. These lines, do, however, present the proper relationship to the other lines of the isometric drawing.

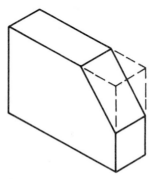

Fig. 14-11 Correctly drawn isometric

ASSIGNMENT

A. Sketching

Refer to drawings in the back of this book, sheet 6/6. Make an isometric sketch of the cabinets at △C in the powder room.

1. It is not necessary to sketch the mirror and light.

2. Assume that the cabinets are 22 inches deep.

3. Refer to the plan view on sheet 3/6 for more information.

4. Let each square on the grid equal 4 inches.

ASSIGNMENT _____   (14)   DR.BY _____   CH.BY _____   RATING _____

Section 4
Elements of Light Construction

UNIT 15   Foundations

OBJECTIVES

After completing this unit, you will be able to:

- explain the functions of footings and foundations.
- identify the basic features of a foundation.

PURPOSE OF A FOUNDATION

The foundation of a building is the portion below the first floor. The foundation for a building supports a heavy load. The heavier the building, the greater the load is on the foundation.

All of the weight of the building, including the foundation, eventually rests on the earth below. Very few types of soil are capable of supporting an entire building on the small area of a typical foundation wall. To spread the weight of the building over a larger area, the foundation walls usually rest on *footings,* figure 15-1. The footings are often about twice as wide as the thickness of the wall. However, the footing design varies according to the weight of the building and strength of the soil.

The depth at which the footings are placed is just as important as their size. Nearly

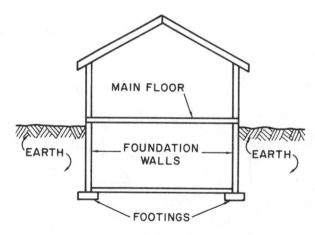

Fig. 15-1 Foundation

all soil contains water. As the water freezes the ground swells. The maximum depth to which ground freezes is called the *frost line,* figure 15-2. To prevent freezing and swelling from damaging the foundation, the footings must be below the frost line.

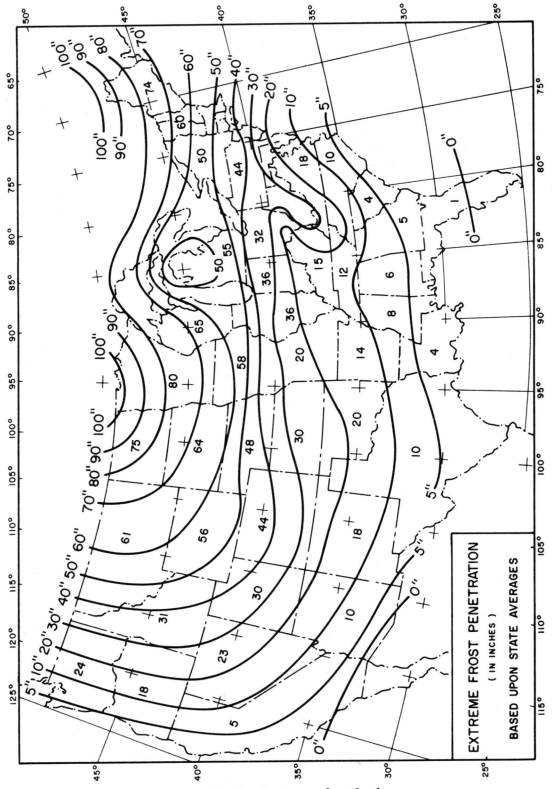

Fig. 15-2 Map showing average frost depths

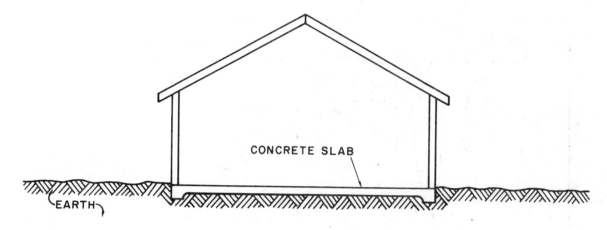

Fig. 15-3 Slab on grade

TYPES OF FOUNDATIONS

There are three types of foundations which are commonly used in small buildings. The simplest to understand is *slab-on-grade* construction, figure 15-3. In this kind of construction, concrete is placed directly on the ground for the first floor. Slab-on-grade (or *mat*) foundations distribute the building load over a very large area. However, this type is only suitable where the ground does not freeze.

Where the frost line is near the surface, the footings may be only a few feet below the surface. In this case, there is not enough space for a full cellar. Usually, however, a crawl space is provided for access to plumbing and wiring, figure 15-4. Crawl-space foundations are also used where there is too much ground water to make a dry basement practical.

In colder regions, the foundation is usually deep enough to allow for a basement. Houses with full basements usually have a water heater and furnace or boiler located in the basement. This design also includes cellar stairs.

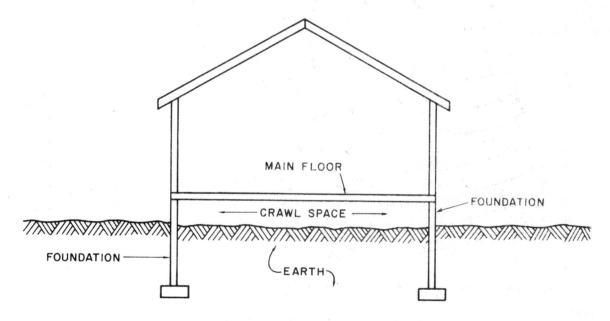

Fig. 15-4 Crawl space

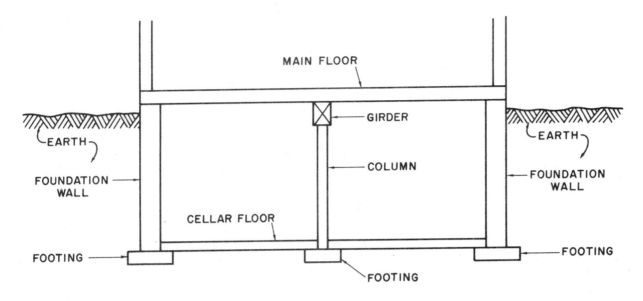

Fig. 15-5 Girders and columns support the floor between the foundation walls

COLUMNS AND GIRDERS

The floor of a building usually requires some support between the foundation walls. This support is provided by girders (wooden or steel beams) and posts or columns, figure 15-5. Girders may be *built up* by nailing several pieces of wood together, box beams made of plywood on a lumber frame, steel laminated plywood beams or solid wood, figure 15-6. The columns or posts which support the girder rest on concrete footings.

MOISTURE CONTROL

In all but very dry soil, some provision is made for keeping moisture out of the basement or crawl space. One common method is to *parge* (plaster) the outside of the foundation with cement, then coat it with asphalt foundation coating.

As water passes through the ground and comes in contact with the asphalt-coated wall, it runs down the wall toward the footing. A plastic or ceramic drain pipe around the footing carries the water away from the building, figure 15-7.

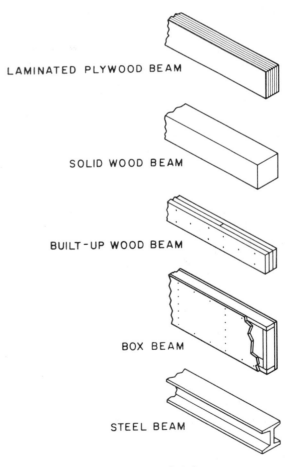

Fig. 15-6   Types of girders

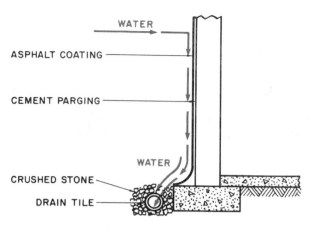

WATER

ASPHALT COATING ——

CEMENT PARGING ——

WATER

CRUSHED STONE —

DRAIN TILE ——

Fig. 15-7 Moisture control

The area of earth beneath the building must be separated from the building by a moisture barrier. Polyethylene (plastic) sheeting is the most common material for this moisture barrier. Before the concrete is placed, whether for a basement floor or the main floor of the building, the entire area is covered with a moisture barrier.

In regions where the earth freezes in winter, thermal insulation may also be placed beneath the slab or around the outside of the foundation walls. Plastic foam boards are usually used for this purpose.

ASSIGNMENT

Questions

1. What part of a building spreads its weight over a larger area of soil?
    The foundation walls on footings ✓

2. What is the most important factor in determining foundation depth?
    below the frost line

3. What two factors affect the dimension of a footing? Weight of building
    and Strength of Soil

4. What is the name of the maximum depth to which the ground freezes?
    the frost line ✓

5. Why is a slab on grade not practical for a house in the north? Needed for heating

6. What supports the floor of a house between the foundation walls?
    Girder, Posts

7. What is the purpose of asphalt foundation coating?
    To keep water out ✓

8. When ground water reaches the footing, how can it be taken away?
    through a drain pipe around the footing

9. When columns support a girder, what do the columns rest on?
    footing ✓

10. Name three types of girders. Solid wood Beam,
    Box Beam, Built up wood Beam.

around 24-inch major modules (six 4-inch modules), figure 16-3. Although it is not always possible to design rooms around the 24-inch module, the overall dimensions of the building are easily held to this standard. With this system, if a 2-foot piece of wall material (1/2 of a 4-foot panel) is leftover at one end of the wall, it can be used on the opposite wall.

WALLS

Walls serve two major functions. They separate spaces — one room from another or indoors from outdoors. They also support the weight of whatever is above them—second floor, ceiling, roof, etc. The *studs* in walls give them strength to support this weight. These vertical members are usually either 2″ x 4″ or 2″ x 6″ lumber. At their tops and bottoms, studs are fastened to *plates*.

Studs also provide a surface on which to attach covering materials. On the exterior, the wall covering is called *sheathing* and may be plywood, fiberboard, or foamed plastic sheets. On the interior, the most common wall coverings are gypsum wallboard and simulated wood paneling.

Additional framing members are used around the openings for doors and windows. A *header* is placed over the top of the opening. The header transfers the load from above the opening to the studs at the sides. These studs are doubled to carry the extra weight. In window openings, a stool is added to frame the bottom of the opening. Figure 16-4 shows the parts of a wall frame.

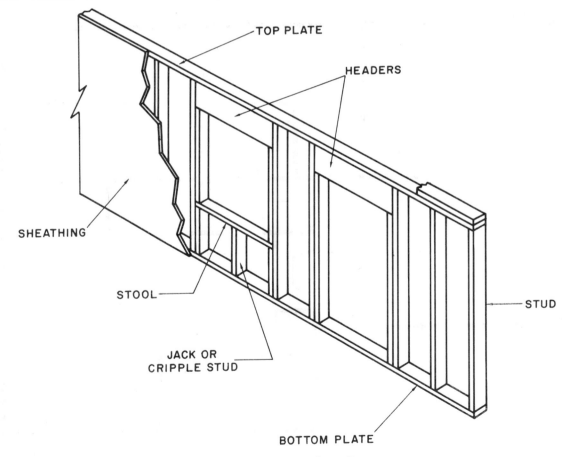

Fig. 16-4 Parts of a wall

FLOORS

Floors are similar to walls in that they are made of evenly spaced framing members which support a covering. In floors the framing members are *joists*. The joists rest on the foundation wall or a girder. The outer ends of the floor joists are joined by a *header joist*. *Bridging* is often added to prevent twisting and springiness in the floor joists. Bridging may be either diagonal pieces of wood or metal, or solid pieces of wood.

Where openings are made for stairs or chimneys, the joists are doubled and a *joist header* supports the ends of short joists.

Floor framing is covered with *subflooring* which is usually plywood. The subfloor is covered with hardwood flooring or underlayment. *Underlayment* adds strength which would otherwise be added by the hardwood flooring. Figure 16-5 shows the parts of a floor. Floors above the first floor are constructed the same, but rest on the lower frame walls instead of the foundation.

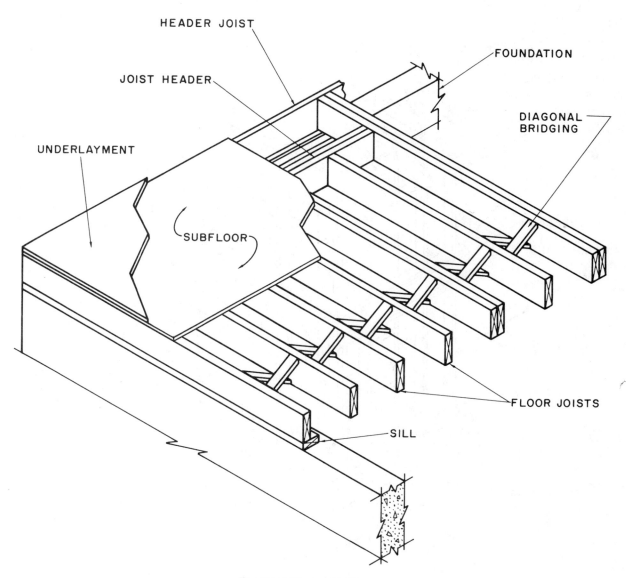

Fig. 16-5 Parts of a floor

CEILINGS

The ceiling is usually the underside of the floor above. In a single story house or the top story of other builidngs, the ceiling may be framed with smalller joists than a floor. Besides providing a surface at the top of the rooms, the ceiling joists prevent the walls from spreading apart.

ROOFS

A discussion of the main elements of frame construction would not be complete without including roof framing. The obvious function of a roof is to protect the building from the weather. Roof construction is explained in Unit 17. Figure 16-6 shows the relationship of the major parts of a building frame.

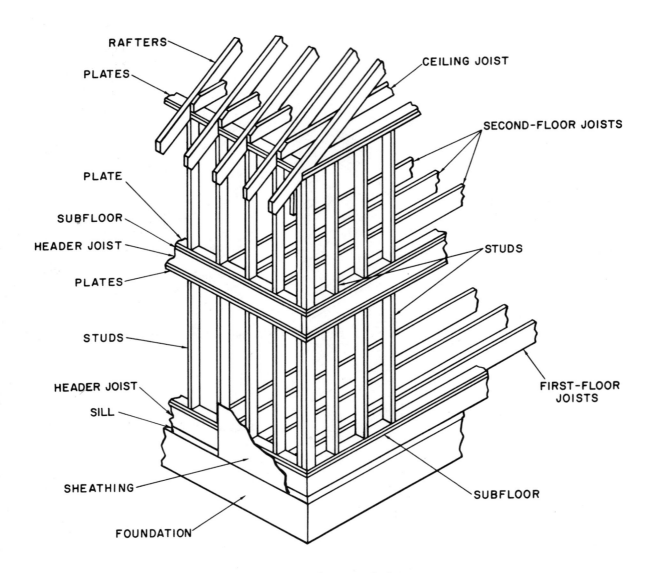

Fig. 16-6 Main elements of a house

ENERGY-EFFICIENT CONSTRUCTION

Recently, construction systems have been developed to conserve energy. Most of these are intended to collect the sun's heat or to prevent the passage of heat through the building's surfaces. Developments in wall framing have mostly been intended to reduce the loss of heat in winter or the gain of heat in the summer.

When wall framing is done with 2 x 4s spaced 16 inches on centers, a fairly large amount of solid wood is exposed to the surface of the wall. Wood conducts heat out of the building. Only the space between the solid wood framing can be filled with insulation. By using 2 x 6 studs spaced 24 inches on centers, the area of solid wood exposed to the surface of the wall is reduced by 20 percent, figure 16-7. The amount of framing material is the same. Not only does this reduce the amount of wood exposed to the surface of the wall, but it also allows for 2 inches more insulation.

In the past it has been conventional to use three studs to construct a corner in a wall, figure 16-8. Another method for reducing the area of exposed wood is by using a 2-piece

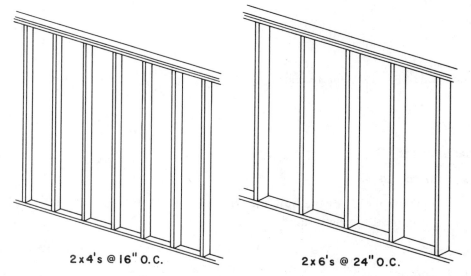

2x4's @ 16" O.C.   2x6's @ 24" O.C.

Fig. 16-7 Using 2 x 6 studs spaced 24" center to center (24" O.C.) reduces the amount of wood exposed to the surface of the wall.

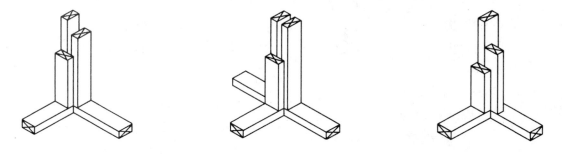

Fig. 16-8 Conventional corner posts for 2 x 4 framing

corner construction, figure 16-9. The third piece, which normally provides a nailing surface for the interior wallboard, is replaced by metal clips. Also, in energy-efficient construction, trussed headers are used, figure 16-10.

Many modern construction materials have been developed to make buildings more energy efficient. For example, the use of insulating sheathing instead of plywood can add as much insulating value as that found within a conventional 2 x 4 wall frame.

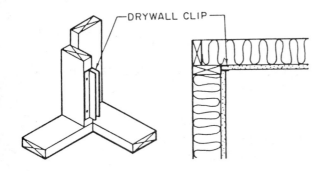

Fig. 16-9 Two-piece corner construction

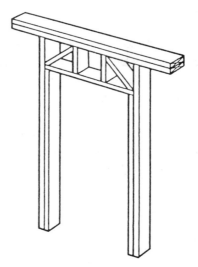

Fig. 16-10 Trussed header

ASSIGNMENT

A. Matching

Indicate which of the building parts in the left-hand column is described by each item in the right-hand column.

a. Joist	__E__	1. Transfers the weight from above to the sides of an opening
b. Header joist	__B__	2. Nailed to the ends of the floor joists
c. Stud	__F__	3. Nailed to the top of the floor joists
d. Bridging	__A__	4. Main framing members in a floor
e. Header	__C__	5. Main framing members in a wall
f. Subfloor	__D__	6. Diagonal bracing in a floor
g. Top plate	__I__	7. Exterior wall covering
h. Underlayment	__J__	8. Interior wall covering
i. Sheathing	__H__	9. Applied over first layer of flooring instead of hardwood
j. Gypsum wallboard	__G__	10. Nailed to tops of studs

UNIT 17   Roof Framing

OBJECTIVES

After completing this unit, you will be able to:

- identify the most common types of roofs used on residences.
- explain the function of roof-framing members.

The roof of a house protects the structure and its occupants from rain and snow. The roof must be capable of supporting a heavy load, especially where several feet of snow may fall on the roof.

TYPES OF ROOFS

There are five types of roofs that are commonly used in residential construction, figure 17-1. Variations of these may be used to create certain architectural styles.

Gable Roof. The *gable roof* is one of the most common types used on houses. The gable roof consists of two sloping sides which meet at the ridge. The triangle formed at the ends of the house between the top plates of the wall and roof is called the *gable*.

Gambrel Roof. The *gambrel roof* is similar to the gable roof. On this roof, the sides slope very steeply from the walls to a point about halfway up the roof, then they have a more gradual slope.

Hip Roof. The *hip roof* slopes on all four sides. The hip roof has no exposed wall above the top plates. This results in all four sides of the

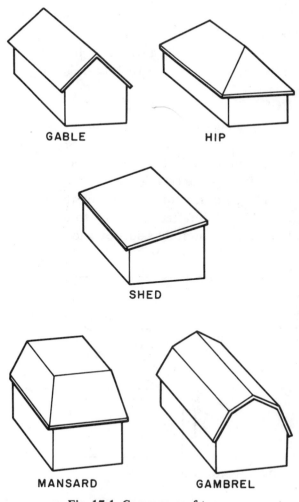

Fig. 17-1 Common roof types

house being equally protected from the weather.

Mansard Roof. The *Mansard roof* is similar to the hip roof, except the lower half of the roof has a very steep slope and the top half is more gradual. This roof style is used extensively in commercial construction, such as on stores.

Shed Roof. The *shed roof* is a simple sloped roof with no ridge. Although the shed roof is not as common as other types for residential construction, it is used on some modern houses and additions to houses.

CONVENTIONAL RAFTER FRAMING

The roof-framing members that extend from the wall plates to the ridge are called *common rafters*. On a shed roof the common rafters span the entire structure.

ROOF-FRAMING TERMS

The main parts in a roof above the ceiling joists are the rafters and the ridgeboard. The *ridgeboard* runs the length of the roof between the rafters of the two sides. The ridgeboard is a nailing surface for the tops of the rafters.

When the rafters are ready to be cut, the first one is carefully laid out and used as a pattern. To discuss rafters, a few terms must be understood, figure 17-2.

- *Span* is the total width to be covered by the rafters. This is usually the distance between the outside walls of the house.

- *Run* is the width covered by one rafter. If the roof has the same slope on both sides, the run is one-half the span.

- *Rise* is the height from the top of the wall plates to the top of the roof.

- *Measuring line* is an imaginary line along the center of the rafter. This is where the length of the rafter is measured.

- *Plumb cuts* are the cuts made at the top and bottom of each rafter. These cuts are plumb (vertical) when the rafter is in place.

- *Tail* is the portion of the rafter that extends from the wall outward to create the *overhang* at the eaves.

- *Pitch* is the steepness of the roof. This is usually expressed in terms of the number of inches of rise per foot of run. For example, if the height of the roof changes 4 inches for every 12 inches horizontally, the pitch is referred to as 4 in 12.

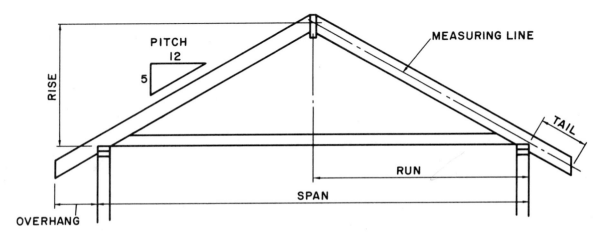

Fig. 17-2 Roof-framing terms

12	11	10	9	8	7	6	5	4	3	2
16 97	16 28	15 62	15	14 42	13 89	13 42	13	12 65	12 37	12 16
20 78	20 22	19 70	19 21	18 76	18 36	18	17 69	17 44	17 23	17 09
22 5/8	21 11/16	20 13/16	20	19 1/4	18 1/2	17 7/8	17 5/16	16 7/8	16 1/2	16 1/4
33 15/16	32 9/16	31 1/4	30	28 7/8	27 3/4	28 13/16	26	25 5/16	24 3/4	24 5/16
8 1/2	8 7/8	9 1/4	9 5/8	10	10 3/8	10 3/4	11 1/16	11 3/8	11 5/8	11 13/16
9 7/8	0 1/8	10 3/8	10 5/8	10 7/8	11 1/16	11 5/16	11 1/2	11 11/16	11 13/16	11 15/16

Fig. 17-3 Rafter table on the face of a square. The top line of the table is the length of common rafters per foot of run.

RAFTER TABLES

Carpenters use rafter tables to determine the length of the rafters. These tables are available in handbooks and are usually printed on framing squares, figure 17-3. To find the length of a common rafter:

Step 1 Find the number of inches of rise per foot of run at the top of the table. These numbers are the regular graduations on the square.

Step 2 Under this number, find the length of the rafter per foot of run. A space between the numbers indicates a decimal point.

Step 3 Multiply the length of the common rafter per foot of run (the number found in step 2) by the number of feet of run.

Step 4 Add the length of the tail and subtract one-half the thickness of the ridge-board. The result is the length of the common rafter as measured along the measuring line.

Note: If the overhang is given on the working drawings, it can be added to the run of the rafter instead of adding the length of the tail.

Example: Find the length of a common rafter for the roof in figure 17-4. (Refer to the rafter table in figure 17-3.

1. *Rise per foot of run = 4"*

2. *Length of common rafter per foot of run = 12.65"*

3. *Run of one rafter including overhang = 16'-0"*

4. *16 x 12.65" = 202.40" (round off to 202 1/2")*

5. *Subtract 1/2 the thickness of the ridge-board: 202 1/2" - 3/4" = 201 3/4"*

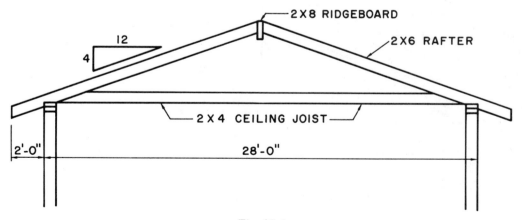

Fig. 17-4

TRUSSED RAFTERS

Through engineering advances, a system has been devised that speeds roof framing, reduces material needs, and produces stronger roofs. This is the use of trussed rafters. Trussed rafters, commonly called *roof trusses,* are units assembled in a shop. These units are then transported to the construction site and set on the walls, figure 17-5.

This is the system of roof construction used most often today. The top members of a truss, corresponding to rafters, are the *top chords.* The *bottom chord* is on the bottom of the truss and corresponds to the ceiling joists in conventional rafter framing. Depending on the design of the truss, there are several braces, called *webs,* between the top and bottom chords. The parts of the truss are held together with plywood or metal plates, called *gussets.*

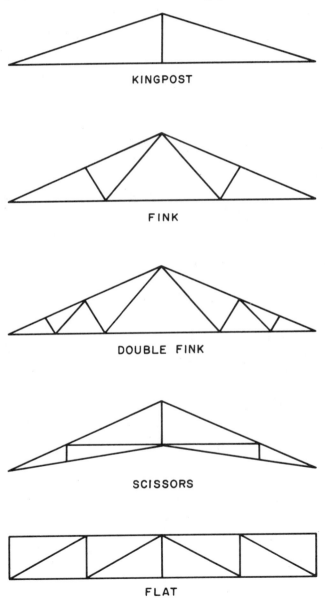

KINGPOST

FINK

DOUBLE FINK

SCISSORS

FLAT

Fig. 17-5 Some common types of roof trusses

GABLE FRAMING

Whether conventional framing or roof trusses are used, the triangular ends of a gable roof must be filled in with framing. If the architect specifies a trussed roof, gable trusses are set on the end walls. In conventional framing, gable-end studs are placed directly above the regular wall studs. Gable-end studs are toenailed to the top wall plate and notched to fit against the end rafter.

RAKE FRAMING

When the roof overhangs at the ends, special framing is required. This involves the use of *gable plates* and *lookouts*. The overhanging rafter is nailed to the ends of the lookouts. The lookouts rest on top of the gable plates, figure 17-6.

The final member of the roof frame is the *fascia header*. This is a piece of lumber the same size as the rafters nailed to the ends of the rafters. The fascia header will support trim to be added later.

ROOF COVERING

Most types of roof coverings require that the roof frame be covered with boards or plywood first. This is called the *roof sheathing* or *roof decking*. Roof sheathing is applied over the rafters in the same way that subflooring is applied over the floor joists.

The first step in covering the sheathing is to apply roofing underlayment. *Roofing underlayment* serves two purposes: It prevents chemical reactions between the resins in the wood and the roof covering material; and it provides additional weather protection. Asphalt-saturated felt is the most common roofing underlayment material.

Common roof coverings for residential construction are asphalt-rolled roofing, asphalt shingles, and wood shingles and shakes.

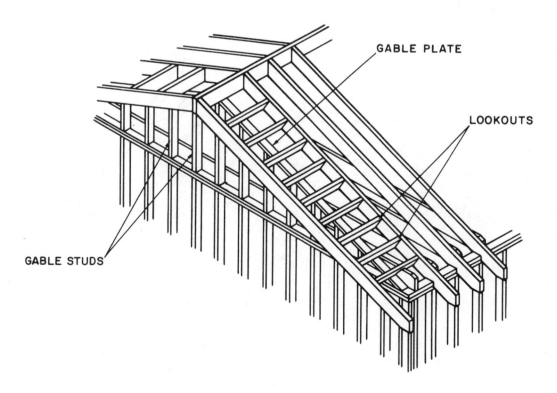

Fig. 17-6 Framing for an overhang at the gable end

Asphalt strip shingles are the most common. Asphalt shingles and rolled roofing are available in several weights. The weight is specified according to the weight of material required to cover one square. (A *square* is 100 square feet of roof.) Underlayment felt is generally a 15-pound weight. Strip shingles are generally 225- to 240-pound asphalt.

ASSIGNMENT

A.   Identification

Show where these items are indicated in the illustrations of a conventional roof and a trussed rafter.

7 Top chord ✓

1 Common rafter ✓

2 Ridgeboard ✓

6 Web member ✓

9 Gusset ✓

3 Gable stud ✓

8 Bottom chord ✓

10 Span ✓

5 Tail ✓

4 Fascia header ✓

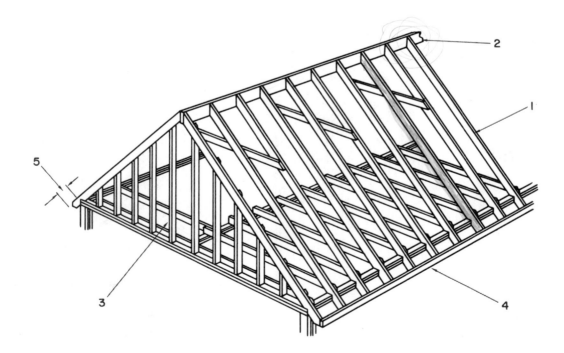

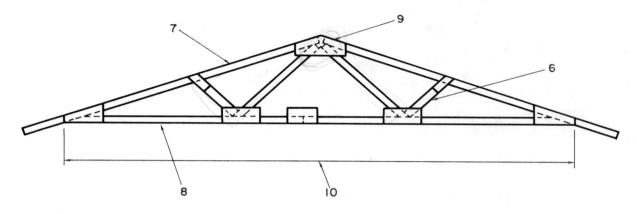

B. Completion

1. The height from the top of the wall plates to the top of the roof is the
    rise. ✓

2. The total width covered by a pair of rafters is the ~~FLA.~~ span ✓

3. The width covered by a single rafter is the run. ✓

4. The imaginary line along which a rafter is measured is the measuring line ✓

5. The portion of a rafter that extends outside the wall plate is the overhang
    tail ✓

6. The steepness of a roof is the Pitch. ✓

7. A rafter which extends all the way from the wall plate to the ridgeboard
    is called a gable. plate x Common Rafter

Section 5
Reading Construction Drawings

UNIT 18   Plot Plans

OBJECTIVES

After completing this unit, you will be able to:

- identify features indicated on a plot plan.
- interpret boundary markings on a plot plan.
- interpret contour markings on a plot plan.
- interpret dimensions on a plot plan.

The work to be done on a building site and the location of the building is as important as the building itself. Before construction of the building begins, the site must be prepared. It may be necessary to add *fill* (soil) to low spots, remove it from high spots, and remove trees, etc. The plans for this work are communicated by use of a *plot plan*. The plot plan fully describes the site.

BOUNDARY DESCRIPTION

The first step in surveying a piece of property is to establish the *point of beginning* (POB). This may be called a *datum* or *bench mark* (BM). The point of beginning may be any stationary object, such as a manhole

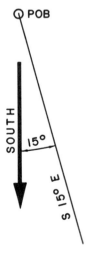

Fig. 18-1   A line 15 degrees east of due south has a bearing of S 15° E.

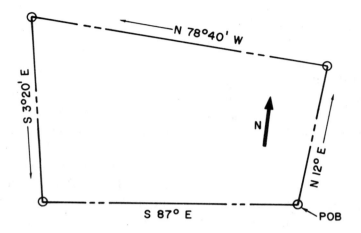

Fig. 18-2 Angles of less than one degree are given in minutes.

cover, iron pin, or existing building. The point of beginning is shown on the plot plan.

The direction and dimension of each boundary is measured from this point. A system of *bearings* is used to indicate direction. A bearing is given as a number of degrees east or west from a north or south line. For example, a line 15 degrees east of due south has a bearing of S 15° E, figure 18-1. Angles of less than one degree are measured in minutes (abbreviated by '), figure 18-2. There are 60 minutes in a degree. A line 20 1/2 degrees west of due north has a bearing of N 20°30′ W.

CONTOUR

The height of a point is shown as an *elevation*. This is the number of feet above a particular reference point. The most common reference point for elevation is sea level, but it can be the surface of a nearby lake or a permanent monument erected by the city, town, or county. The elevation is given at each corner of the site, figure 18-3.

To describe the contour of the site, or rise and fall, a system of contour lines is used. These lines follow the surface of the land at a particular elevation. These lines are spaced at

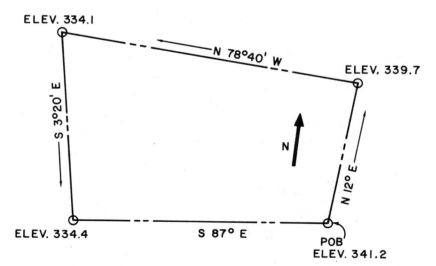

Fig. 18-3 The highest corner on this site is the point of beginning.

regular intervals of elevation, usually one foot. On a steep slope the lines are close together. On a gradual slope they are farther apart, figure 18-4.

If the contour of the site is to be changed, both the existing, or *natural* grade is shown by solid contour lines. The finished grade is shown by broken contour lines.

LOCATING THE BUILDING

The plot plan indicates where the building is to be located on the site. The basic shape of the building and its overall dimensions are given. The distances from the front and at least one side boundary are also given. In ad-

dition, the elevation of the first floor is included on the plot plan.

OTHER FEATURES

Anything else that provides useful information about the site is included on the plot plan. Walks, drives, and patios are shown with their dimensions. If there are other buildings on the site they are included. Trees are shown by symbols and any that are to be removed are marked. Utilities, such as water mains, sewers, and electric power lines, are shown by phantom lines. To help orient the plot plan, a bold arrow shows the direction of north.

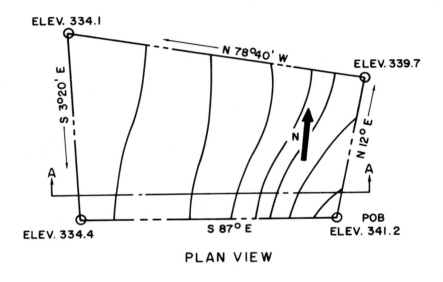

PLAN VIEW

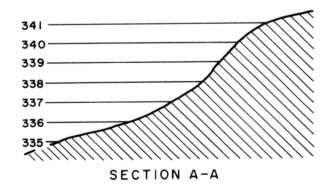

SECTION A-A

Fig. 18-4 The contour is shown with contour lines on the plot plan.

ASSIGNMENT

Questions

Refer to the drawings in the back of the textbook to answer the following questions.

1. What is the distance from the front boundary to the front of the house?

   80'-0"

2. What is the length of each boundary line?

   North   124'-6"

   South   140'-0"

   East   150'-0"

   West   140'-0"

3. What is the highest elevation on the site?   101

4. What is the elevation where the walk meets the house?   100.4

5. What is the elevation at the northwest corner of the house?   97'

6. How wide is the concrete walk?   3'-0"

7. What are the overall dimensions of the house, excluding the garage and terrace?   30'-0" - 56'-6"

8. What utility services are available near the site?   Elec, sewer, H₂O

9. At which end of the house is the slope of the site steepest?   North-West

10. What is the difference in height from the garage floor to the house floor?   1.2

11. In what general direction will rain water run off the site when it falls from the roof of the house?   North-West

12. At approximately what elevations are the two individual trees?   99.5 / 100.50

UNIT 19 Foundation Plans

OBJECTIVES

After completing this unit, you will be able to:

- identify features shown on a foundation plan.
- interpret dimensions shown on a foundation plan.

The foundation plan, like other plan views in construction, is shown as an imaginary cut through the foundation. It provides complete information for construction below the first floor.

FOUNDATION WALLS AND FOOTINGS

The foundation plan shows the dimensions of the foundation walls. The material of which the foundation is made is included in a note or by use of the proper section symbol. Most foundations are concrete or concrete block. Dimensions are included for the overall width and length, thickness, and the location of all features. Complete information about the location of intersecting walls and other prominent features is included, figure 19-1.

Some foundation plans show the footing with a hidden line. These plans may include a note giving the size of the footing. However, because local building codes often specify the size of the footing, the code should be checked in all cases.

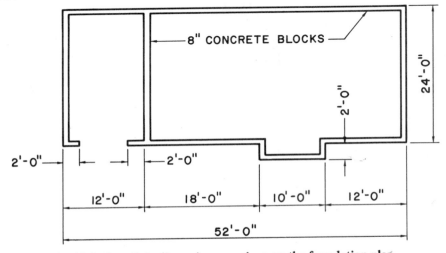

Fig. 19-1 Complete dimensions are given on the foundation plan.

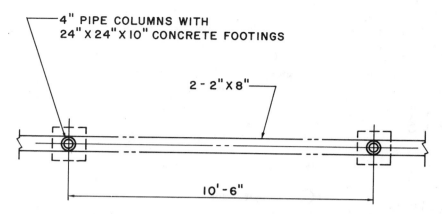

Fig. 19-2 Columns and girders are shown on the foundation plan.

COLUMNS AND GIRDERS

Most buildings include at least one girder resting on columns or masonry piers to support the first floor. These are shown on the foundation plan. Girders are shown by phantom lines with a note to indicate size and type. If the girder is supported by columns or posts, these are shown by a small circle. If the girder is supported by piers, they are shown by rectangles. In either case, their location is dimensioned to their centerlines. Each column, post, or pier rests on a footing which is shown on the foundation plan, figure 19-2.

FLOOR JOISTS

The size, direction, and spacing of joists is given on the plan for the space below. This means that information for the first-floor joists is shown on the foundation plan. This is customarily given by an arrow showing the direction and a note indicating the size and OC (On Center) spacing, figure 19-3. Where partitions above carry part of the weight of the building, the floor joists are usually doubled.

OTHER STRUCTURAL FEATURES

If the design of the building includes a cellar, the foundation plan includes stairs, windows, and doors. Some of these features may require more detail than can be shown on a typical foundation plan. Detail drawings which show this information are covered in Unit 22. However, the foundation plan includes dimensions for the location of these features.

Notes are included in any convenient uncluttered area to indicate such things as floor treatment and concrete slabs. Typical notes of this type indicate where concrete-slab floors are called for and where excavation is not required.

ELECTRICAL

The floor plans and foundation plans for houses and small commercial buildings usually include the location of electrical devices. The foundation plan may include light fixtures, switches, and the electrical service panel. These devices are shown by

2"X 8" - 16" O C

Fig. 19-3 This indicates that 2" x 8" joists are spaced 16 inches from the center of one to the center of the next.

symbols. Figure 19-4 shows a few typical electrical symbols. Often the drawings include one sheet that lists and explains all of the symbols used on the entire set of drawings.

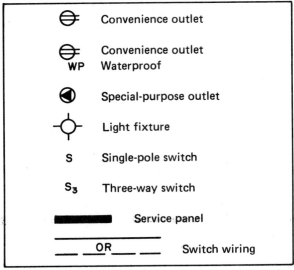

Fig. 19-4 Electrical symbols found on foundation plans

ASSIGNMENT

Questions

Refer to the drawings in the back of the textbook to answer the following questions.

1. What is the overall length of the house including the garage?

   67' ✓

2. What are the overall dimensions of the garage?

   22' - 25'-6" ✓

3. How many 4-inch pipe columns are there?

   6 ✓

4. What size (thickness x width) beams are used for the girders?

   4"x10" ✓

5. What is the main difference between the area on the right end of the house and that on the left end?

   Left colums excavated/un excavated
   Right Piers. excavated

6. How many light fixtures are indicated?

   4 ✓

7. What material are the foundation walls made of?

   Conc. BLOCK ✓

8. What size (thickness x width) are the first-floor joists?

   2"x10" ✓

9. What is the spacing of the first-floor joists?

   16" ✓

10. How wide are the cellar stairs? <u>3'-0"</u> ✓   ✓

11. What are the dimensions of the fireplace footing? <u>2'-10"</u> × 7'-6'

12. How may windows are there in the north wall of the foundation? <u>1</u>

UNIT 20   Floor Plans

OBJECTIVES

After completing this unit, you will be able to:

- identify features shown on a floor plan.
- interpret dimensions shown on a floor plan.
- interpret information given in door and window schedules.

The floor plan is similar to the foundation plan. It is a section of the building at a height that shows the placement of walls, windows, doors, and other important features. A separate floor plan is drawn for each floor of the building.

WALLS AND PARTITIONS

Walls on a floor plan are drawn the same way as for a foundation plan. They are drawn to scale and their exact location is dimensioned. The location may be dimensioned from the centerline or the edge of the wall frame, figure 20-1. Because the carpenters who build the walls usually measure from the surface of the studs and plates, most dimensions are given from the surface of the wall frame.

DOORS

The location, size, and direction of opening (*swing*) are given for doors. Doors are shown on the plan with a symbol showing the swing. A straight line represents the door and an arc represents the swing of the outside edge. Other types of doors are shown by symbols which represent the operation of the door, figure 20-2, page 108.

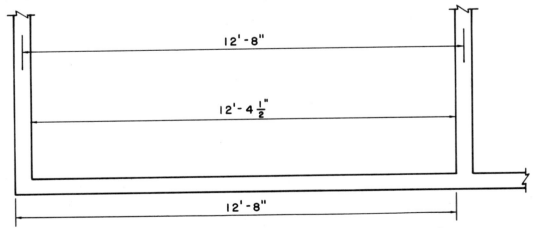

$12'-8"$

$12'-4\frac{1}{2}"$

$12'-8"$

Fig. 20-1 Walls may be dimensioned to their centerline or their surface.

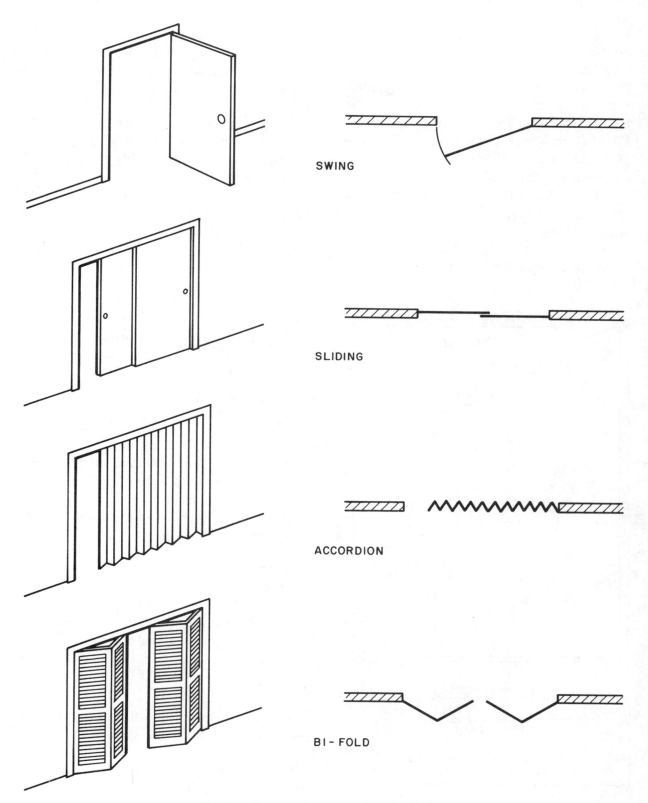

SWING

SLIDING

ACCORDION

BI - FOLD

Fig. 20-2 Types of doors and their plan symbols

Doors are generally available in widths from 2'-0" to 3'-0" in 2-inch increments. The height of most doors in homes is 6'-8", but 7'-0" doors are sometimes used for the main entrance. Interior doors in homes are usually 1 3/8" thick, but exterior doors are usually 1 3/4" thick. The width, height, and thickness of the door is given either on the symbol or in a separate schedule.

Schedules are used to give information that would normally clutter the drawings. When a door schedule is used, doors are labeled with a letter or number. The schedule gives complete information for each type of door, figure 20-3.

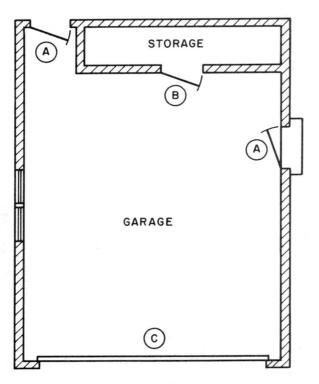

DOOR SCHEDULE

MARK	SIZE	TYPE	REMARKS
A	3'-0" x 6'-8"	2-PANEL	GLAZED
B	3'-0" x 6'-8"	FLUSH	SOLID CORE
C	18'-0" x 7'-0"	OVERHEAD	

Fig. 20-3

WINDOWS

There are basically five types of windows that are commonly found in houses and small commercial buildings. The plan symbol for each is shown in figure 20-4.

The size of the rough opening (RO) into which the window will be set is especially important to the carpenter. However, the glass size and sash opening are also sometimes given, figure 20-5. The sizes for all windows should be checked with the manufacturer's catalog before the opening is framed. Window sizes are given with the width first and the height second. Information about the windows is sometimes given in a schedule.

In wood frame construction, the windows are located by a dimension given to their centerline. In masonry construction, dimensions are given to the edges of the opening.

OTHER FEATURES ON FLOOR PLANS

Plumbing fixtures. Plumbing fixtures are shown on floor plans by standard symbols. These symbols resemble the fixtures they represent. Plumbing fixture symbols do not include dimensions or other information. They are only intended to show the arrangement of the room.

Cabinets. Cabinets are usually included in the kitchen, bathroom, and laundry room. The outline of cabinets is included on the floor plan to show the general arrangement of these rooms. Special detail drawings (Unit 22) give the necessary information to install the cabinets.

Electrical devices. Electrical devices are shown by symbols in the same manner as on the foundation plan. These symbols do not completely describe the wiring of the house, but do show the approximate location of outlets, light fixtures, and switches.

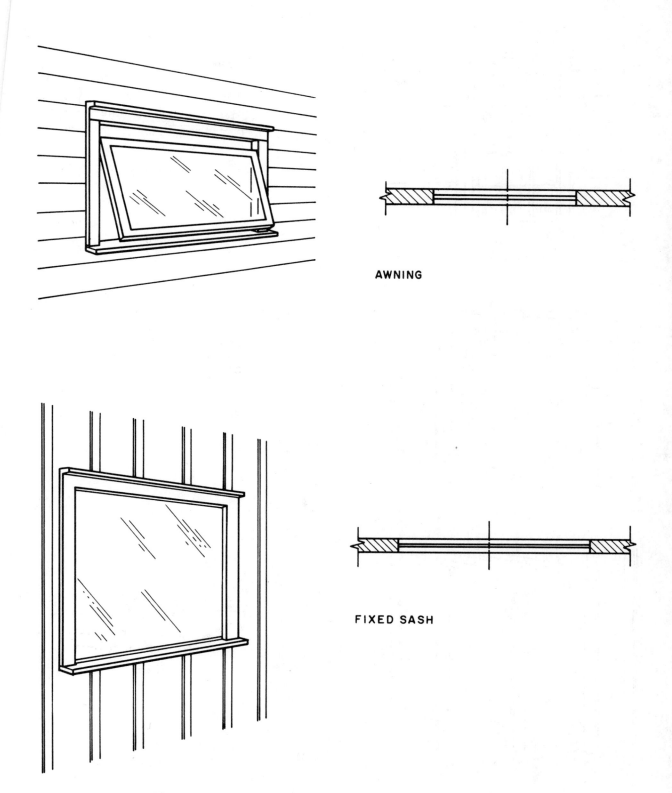

AWNING

FIXED SASH

Fig. 20-4 Types of windows and their plan symbols (Continued)

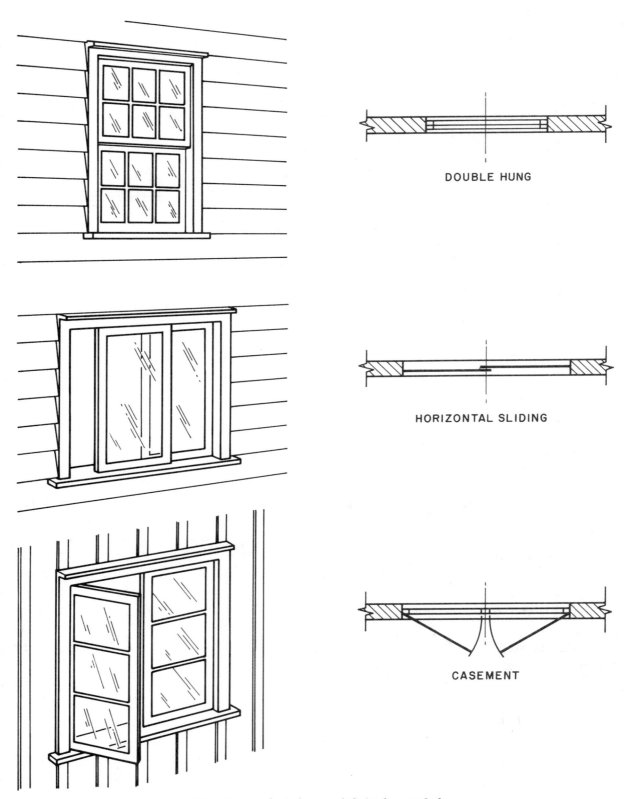

DOUBLE HUNG

HORIZONTAL SLIDING

CASEMENT

Fig. 20-4 Types of windows and their plan symbols

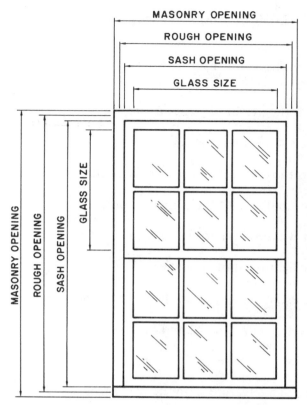

Fig. 20-5 The size of a window can be measured in several ways. The size usually listed is the sash opening.

The floor plans (there will be one for each floor level) are often the most complex drawings in a set of working drawings. The floor plans describe the basic arrangement of rooms and show most of the major features located in each room of the building. The first step in visualizing the building should be an imaginary walk through the plans.

Start at the main entrance and imagine you are looking at the rooms of the house shown in the drawings in the back of this book. As you step off the porch and through the main entrance, you enter the foyer. To the right is the kitchen with a cooking area on the left and a sink on the right. At the far end (east end) of the kitchen is the breakfast area. Back toward the front of the house is the laundry area and a door that leads into the garage. There is one step down to the garage floor. What other features can you identify in the garage? Go back into the kitchen and continue your walk through the house. Take as much time as you need to identify every feature in every room. Look for windows, doors, electrical outlets; everything you can find.

ASSIGNMENT

Questions

Refer to the drawings in the back of the textbook to answer the following questions.

1. What is the overall length of the house including the garage?

    67'-0"

2. What are the inside dimensions of the garage? (Allow 4″ for walls.)

21′-4″ x 21′-2″

3. What are the inside dimensions of the closet in bedroom #2?

2′-6″ x 5′-0

4. How wide is the overhead garage door?

18′-0

5. How many 3′-0″ wide windows are there?

144 Sq In = 1 foot.

18

6. What size is the door at the head of the stairs?

2′-6″ x 6′-8″ x 1 3/8″

7. What is the floor area of the activity room?

365 square fee

8. How many windows cannot be opened?

9

9. How many light fixtures are indicated?

23

10. How wide is the hallway from the foyer to the bedrooms?

3′-4″

11. What separates bedrooms #2 and #3?

Closet + Bathroom

12. Where do the stairs take you?

Basement

13. What outstanding feature is on the north wall of the activity room?

fire Place Chimney

14. How many switches control the light over the vanity in the powder room?

2 (S3)

15. How many 3′-0″ x 6′-8″ x 1 3/8″ doors are there on the main floor?

1

16. How far from the west end of the building is the centerline of the fireplace?

42′-9″

17. How far from the west end of the building is the centerline of the main entrance?

32′4″

18. What is the floor area of the activity room? (Assume all exterior walls are six inches thick and interior partitions are four inches thick.)

351 3″ Sq.Feet
27′-4″ x13′-0″x

19. Based on the plan view of the stairs, what is the distance from the basement floor to the main finished floor?

9′ 3/4 1/2″

20. How many closets or other types of storage rooms are shown on the floor plan?

7

UNIT 21 Elevations

OBJECTIVES

After completing this unit, you will be able to:

- orient exterior elevations to the building plans.
- interpret dimensions, notes, and symbols found on elevations.
- list information typically found on elevations.

GENERAL APPEARANCE

As was previously discussed, an elevation view is any orthographic drawing which shows the height of an object. However, when builders refer to elevations, they generally mean the exterior elevations of a building. A complete set of working drawings includes elevations of all four sides of a building. The elevations are labeled according to their position as you face the front of the building, figure 21-1.

Elevations are usually drawn to the same scale as the floor plans. The line work and symbols used are drawn to resemble the

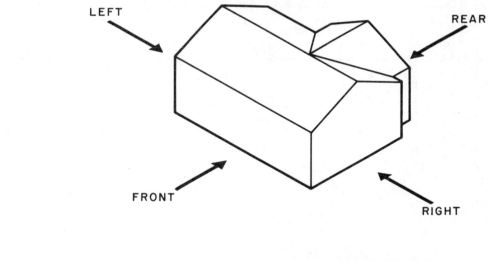

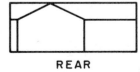

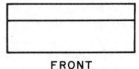
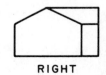

REAR   LEFT   FRONT   RIGHT

Fig. 21-1 Elevation positions

finished building. This allows the person reading the drawings to see what the finished building will look like.

Some architectural features are shown only on the elevations. For example, siding, masonry veneer, and roof covering are indicated by a note on one or more elevations.

FOUNDATION

The elevation drawings show the footing and foundation as hidden lines, figure 21-2. The foundation walls appear as vertical hidden lines. A rectangle at the bottom of the wall indicates the footing.

In some construction not all footings are placed at the same depth. For example, on steeply sloped sites, the footings are *stepped*

to correspond with the grade. This is necessary to keep all footings below the frost line. When a basement is combined with a slab on grade, the footings around the basement may be deeper than around the slab.

WINDOWS AND DOORS

All windows and doors are drawn to resemble their actual appearance on the elevations. Exterior doors are generally either flush or panel doors, figure 21.3. Flush doors are drawn with irregular lines to represent wood grain. Panel doors have rectangles representing the panels. Thin, short diagonal lines indicate glass, called *lites*.

Windows are also drawn as they actually appear. The size may be indicated on the

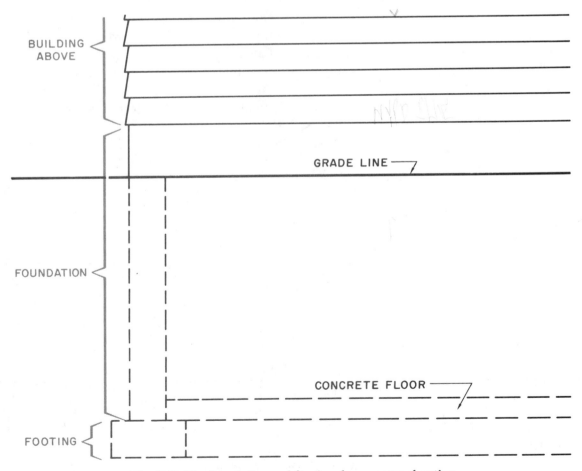

Fig. 21-2 The foundation and footing shown on an elevation

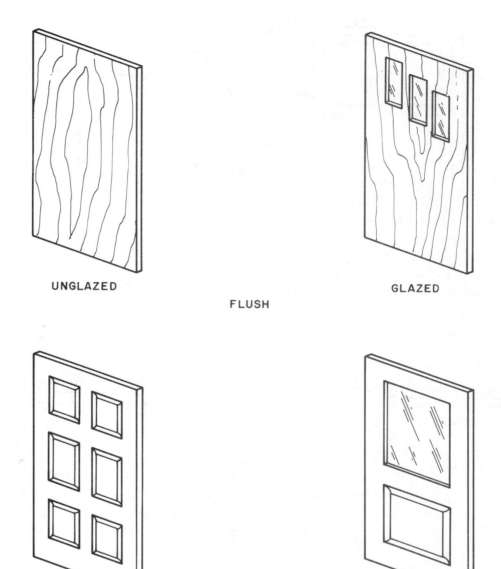

UNGLAZED

GLAZED

FLUSH

6-PANEL UNGLAZED

2-PANEL GLAZED

PANEL

Fig. 21-3 Types of exterior doors

elevation, but it is usually also included on the floor plan or a window schedule. The operation of the window may be shown on the elevations, figure 21-4. Sliding windows are indicated by horizontal arrows. Casement and awning windows have a dashed triangle. The point of the triangle is the hinged side of the window.

DIMENSIONS ON ELEVATIONS

Elevations have only a few dimensions — those that cannot be given on other drawings, figure 21-5. The following are the dimensions included on most elevations:

Floor and ceiling heights. One of the elevations indicates the dimensions from the finished

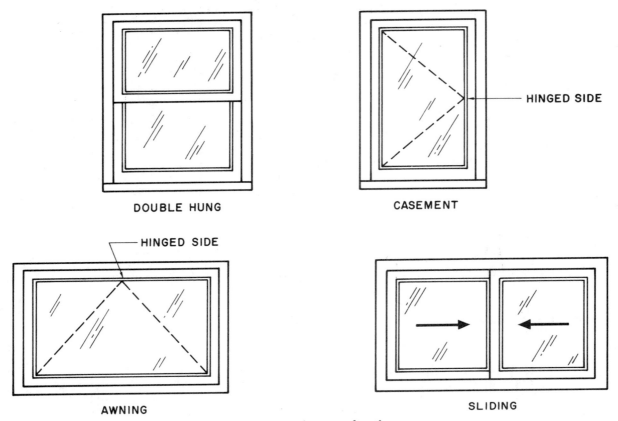

DOUBLE HUNG   CASEMENT

AWNING   SLIDING

Fig. 21-4 Windows on elevations

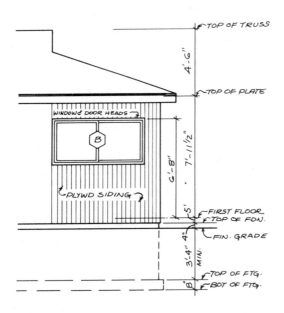

Fig. 21-5 Typical dimensions on a building elevation

grade to the finished floor and from the finished floor to the ceiling. The finished grade is shown by a heavy line. The depth of the basement floor or footings is also given from the finished grade.

Window and door heads. Most doors are a standard height of 6'-8". For uniform appearance, window heads are usually built at the same height as door heads. Because of this standardization, the height of window and door heads may be omitted. However, if any windows are to be set at nonstandard heights, the dimension from the finished floor to the window head (bottom of header) is given on the elevation.

Overhang at eaves. The amount of roof that projects beyond the walls is dimensioned on the elevations. This may not be the same dimension on all sides, so each elevation must be checked.

Roof pitch. The steepness of the roof is called the *pitch*. This is shown on the elevations by a triangular symbol. The pitch symbol includes two numbers. The number on the horizontal side, usually 12", represents a unit of run. The number on the vertical side indicates the amount of rise.

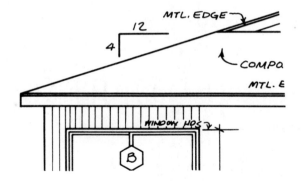

Fig. 21-6 This roof rises 4 inches for every 12 inches horizontally.

Example:
For every 12 inches of run the roof rises 4 inches. This may be stated as 4 $\frac{12}{\diagdown}$

ASSIGNMENT

Questions

Refer to the drawings in the back of the textbook to answer the following questions.

1. What is the pitch of the garage roof?

   Rise 7 / Run 12

2. Why is the footing under the right end of the house not as deep as the footing under the left end?

   Because the ground is higher (unexcavated)

3. What type windows are indicated for the main floor?

   Hinged (casement)

4. Looking at the front elevation, the garage roof overhangs the right end of the house. How much is this overhang?

   16"

5. How much headroom is there in the basement?

   8'-0"

6. How many windows are indicated in the basement?

   3

7. How many doors are shown on the elevations?

   1 front 2 Right + Garage 12/3

8. What is the pitch of the roof over bedroom #2?

9. What material is indicated for the foundation?

   8" Block + Stucco

10. In what part of the house are screened, louvered vents installed overhead?

    3 left elevation (Garage)

11. What is the overhang of the garage roof at the front of the garage?

    12"

12. In what room are the upper windows that are shown at the right end of the front elevation?

    Activity Room

UNIT 22   Details

OBJECTIVES

After completing this unit, you will be able to:

• reference detail drawings to plans and elevations.

• interpret information given on detail drawings.

Not all of the necessary information about a building can be shown on regular plans and elevations. Objects which are too small to be drawn in complete detail on normal floor plans and building elevations are shown on large-scale detail drawings. Construction which is normally hidden from view is shown in section views. These large-scale and section drawings are called *details*. A set of working drawings usually includes several details.

REFERENCING

The first step in reading a detail drawing is to determine what part of the construction it shows. Details are used to show special construction that might not otherwise be understood. Some details may be labeled as typical. This means that the construction shown is used in several places in the construction project. Figure 22-1 is a detail of a typical door head. This construction is used for all sliding doors in the building. Most sets of working drawings include at least one typical wall section. When a section through the entire building is included, the wall section may be omitted.

Details that refer to only one place are identified by some mark on the drawing. As was pointed out in Unit 3, the section views are usually referenced by a cutting-plane line. This heavy line with arrows shows where the imaginary cut was made and from which direction it is viewed.

Reference marks for other details vary from one architect to another. It is important, although not usually difficult, to study the drawings and learn how the architect references details. One common method is with letters or numbers enclosed in triangles, figure 22-2.

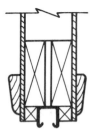

TYPICAL SLIDING DOOR HEAD

SCALE $1\frac{1}{2}$" = 1'-0"

Fig. 22-1

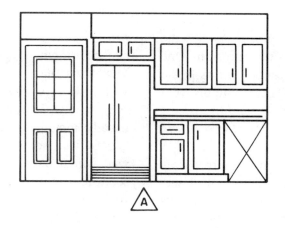

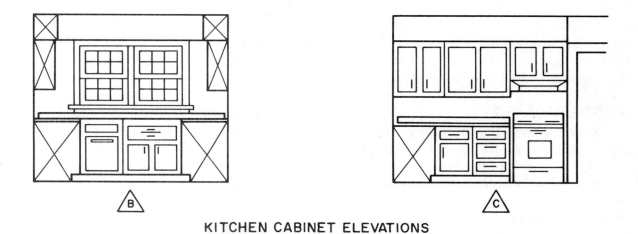

KITCHEN CABINET ELEVATIONS

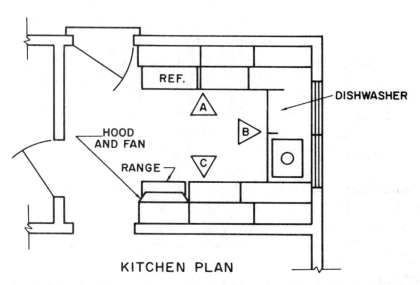

KITCHEN PLAN

Fig. 22-2 Each elevation is drawn as it would be seen by a person standing at the triangles on the plan.

SYMBOLS

Details must be clear enough to give the necessary information without confusion. One technique for simplifying section views is the use of material symbols. These symbols were discussed in Unit 8.

SCALE

Details are usually drawn at a larger scale than regular plans and elevations. Wall sections and other sections which show large parts of the building are usually the smallest scale of the details. They may be as small as 3/8" = 1'-0". Details of small, complex parts are sometimes as large as 3" = 1'-0", figure 22-3. Occasionally there may be a conflict between drawings. In this case, the largest scale drawing should be considered correct.

STANDARD DETAILS

Detail drawings and section views are included for any part of the construction project that requires more information than can be shown in other drawings. There are a few items that are shown in detail drawings with most sets of working drawings.

At least one typical wall section is usually included, figure 22-4. This is called a *typical* wall section, because it describes any wall which does not have a separate, special section. The wall section shows the size of the framing members, insulation, and construction at the top and bottom of the wall.

If there are stairs in the building, there will be one or more detail drawings to show their construction, figure 22-5. Stair details show the height of risers, depth of treads, and how the stairs attach to the rest of the building.

Kitchen cabinet and bathroom vanity elevations are also frequently included on the sheet with details and sections. These elevations show the arrangement of cabinets.

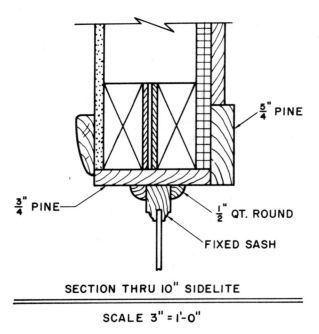

SECTION THRU 10" SIDELITE

SCALE 3" = 1'-0"

Fig. 22-3 Large-scale section view

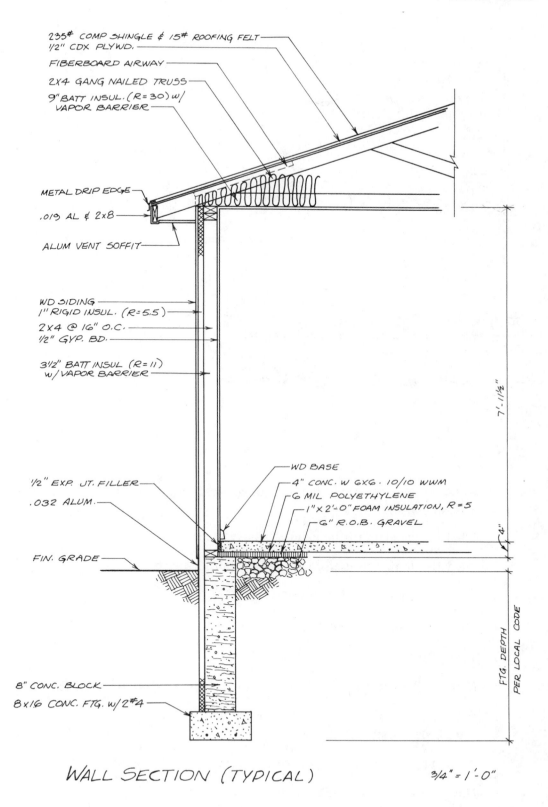

235# COMP SHINGLE & 15# ROOFING FELT
1/2" CDX PLYWD.
FIBERBOARD AIRWAY
2X4 GANG NAILED TRUSS
9" BATT INSUL. (R=30) w/ VAPOR BARRIER
METAL DRIP EDGE
.019 AL & 2x8
ALUM VENT SOFFIT
WD SIDING
1" RIGID INSUL. (R=5.5)
2X4 @ 16" O.C.
1/2" GYP. BD.
3 1/2" BATT INSUL (R=11) w/ VAPOR BARRIER
1/2" EXP. JT. FILLER
.032 ALUM.
FIN. GRADE
WD BASE
4" CONC. W 6X6 · 10/10 WWM
6 MIL POLYETHYLENE
1" X 2'-0" FOAM INSULATION, R=5
6" R.O.B. GRAVEL
8" CONC. BLOCK
8x16 CONC. FTG. w/2#4
7'-11 1/2"
4"
FTG. DEPTH PER LOCAL CODE

WALL SECTION (TYPICAL)   3/4" = 1'-0"

Fig. 22-4 Wall section (typical)

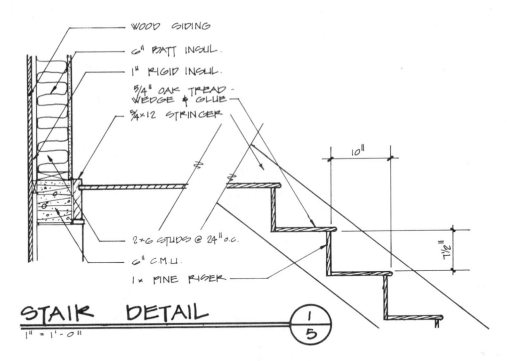

WOOD SIDING
6" BATT INSUL.
1" RIGID INSUL.
5/4" OAK TREAD - WEDGE & GLUE
3/4×12 STRINGER
2×6 STUDS @ 24" o.c.
6" C.M.U.
1× PINE RISER
10"
7½"

STAIR DETAIL

1" = 1'-0"

1/5

Fig. 22-5   Stair detail

ASSIGNMENT

Questions

Refer to the drawings in the back of the textbook to answer the following questions.

1. What is the height of the handrail above the stairs? 2'-6" ✓

2. What size lumber is used to frame the stair landing? 2"×10" ✓

3. What is the spacing of the roof rafters? 16" ✓

4. What is the size of the concrete footing? According to Code

5. What size sill rests on the foundation? 2"×6" ✓

6. How much overhang is there at the eaves of the steep roof? 1'4" ✓

7. What is used for a header over the fixed windows at the top of the activity room? 2-2×8" ✓

8. What supports the top end of the rafters over the kitchen? Let in 1"×4" ✓

9. How many 24" wide x 36" high cabinets are required? 2 ✓

10. What is directly beneath the concrete slab in the basement? 2" rigid insulation ✓

UNIT 23   Specifications

OBJECTIVES

After completing this unit, you will be able to:

- define specifications.
- describe the relationship between working drawings and specifications.
- interpret information found in construction specifications.

PURPOSE OF SPECIFICATIONS

When a set of working drawings for a building is made, it is impossible to include all of the information necessary to build the structure. For example, if the plans show wood floors, they might be oak, maple, or vertical grain fir. Tile flooring on the plans might be ceramic tile, asphalt tile, or vinyl tile. Where the plans show flashing, it could be galvanized steel, aluminum, or copper. Roof shingles can be asphalt or wood. The types of materials used and the quality of these materials must be described in some way.

Information that cannot be clearly shown on the drawings is conveyed to the builder by written specifications. The working drawings for a building give the shape, size, and location. Specifications describe the quality and type of materials, colors, finishes, and workmanship required.

The specifications become a distinct part of the contract. Once the contract has been signed, the specifications cannot be changed. Any corrections that must be made in the specifications after this point must be accompanied by a *change order*. In the case of a dispute between the drawings and the specifications, the specifications should be followed.

Specifications are prepared by the architect or engineer and cover the entire project. The amount of detail and the exact form of the specifications may vary. Specifications serve several purposes:

- They make up a legal document that gives instructions for bids, owner-contractor agreements, insurance, and bond forms that are necessary.
- They help prevent disputes between the builder and the owner, or between the contractor and the architect.
- They eliminate conflicting opinions about the quality of the material to be used.
- They help the contractor estimate the material and labor.
- Together with the working drawings, they are necessary to complete the contract.
- Specifications are part of a legal document.

To make a complete set of specifications for each new job would be unnecessarily time consuming. Instead, specification writers rely on various references for standard specifications from which they compile a set for each new job.

DIVISIONS OF SPECIFICATIONS

In general, specifications for a residence are broken down into divisions that cover work by the different trades. It is standard practice to write the specifications in the order in which the house will be constructed. This makes it easier for the estimator to write a material list and for the contractor and sub-contractors to locate specifications for their particular trade, material, or work.

The following are typical divisions of specifications for a residence:

General Conditions

Excavating and Backfill

Grading

Concrete

Masonry

Carpentry and Millwork

Sheet Metal and Roofing

Glass

Painting

Hardware

Heating and Air Conditioning

Plumbing

Electrical

GENERAL CONDITIONS

In order for the contract to provide complete protection to the parties involved, the specifications include General Conditions, such as the following:

- The contract form
- Supervision of the contract
- The architect's responsibility
- The contractor's responsibility for furnishing the lot lines and any restrictions
- Protection of the work in progress
- The following of manufacturers' instructions
- Quality of workmanship

This section usually mentions the fact that where manufacturers' trade names are listed, it is done to serve as a guide for quality and is not to restrict competitive bidding. Any work or materials not covered elsewhere in the specifications are normally covered in the General Conditions.

TECHNICAL DIVISIONS

Following the General Conditions, the specifications are arranged in divisions according to the work covered. These divisions are generally in the order in which the work is performed. They include all information about grade of materials, quality of workmanship, colors and finishes, etc., that cannot be shown on the drawings. A typical division of specifications follows.

DIVISION 6: CARPENTRY AND MILLWORK

A.   Materials

1.   All materials are to be the best of their respective kind. Lumber shall bear the mark and grade of the association under whose rules it is produced. Framing lumber shall be thoroughly seasoned with a maximum moisture content of 19 percent. All millwork shall be kiln dried.

2. Properly protect all materials. All lumber shall be kept under cover at the job site. Material shall not be delivered unduly long before it is required for work.

3. Lumber for various uses shall be as follows: Framing: No. 2 dimension, Douglas fir or yellow pine. Exterior Millwork: No. 1 clear white pine. The lumber must be sound, thoroughly seasoned, well manufactured, and free from warp which cannot be corrected by bridging or nailing. All woodwork which is exposed to view shall be S4S.

B. Installation

1. All work shall be done by skilled workers.

2. All work shall be erected plumb, true, square, and in accordance with the drawings.

3. Finish work shall be blind nailed as much as possible, and surface nails shall be set.

4. All work shall be securely nailed to studs, nailing blocks, grounds, furring, and nailing strips.

C. Grades and species of lumber

1. Framing lumber, except studs and wall plates, shall be No. 1 Douglas fir.

2. Studs, shoes, and double wall plates shall be Douglas fir, utility grade.

3. Bridging shall be 1" x 3" spruce.

4. Joists shall be spaced 16" OC except where otherwise indicated. All joints are to be doubled under partitions and around stairways and fireplace openings.

5. Subflooring shall be plywood APA grade CDX.

6. Ceiling joists and rafters shall be spaced 16" OC. Rafters are to have overhang as noted on drawings.

7. Roof sheathing shall be 1/2" x 4' x 8' plywood APA grade CD Exterior.

8. Moldings are to be clear pine.

9. Drywall material shall be 1/2" thick gypsum wallboard.

10. Interior woodwork shall be kiln-dried clear pine. All interior woodwork is to be machine sanded at the mill and hand sanded on the job.

11. Hardwood flooring shall be 1" x 3" select oak.

12. Underlayment shall be 5/8" x 4' x 8' particleboard underlayment.

D. Workmanship

1. Framing: All framing members shall be substantially and accurately fitted together, well secured, braced, and nailed. Plates and sills shall be halved together at all corners and splices. Studs in walls and partitions shall be doubled at all corners and openings. Joists over 8′ in span shall be bridged with one row of cross bridging, nailed up tight after the subfloor has been laid.

2. Gypsum wallboard: Gypsum wallboard shall be nailed to wood framing in strict accordance with the manufacturer's recommendation. Space nails not more than 7″ apart on ceilings and not more than 8″ apart on sidewalls. Dimple the nailheads slightly below the surface of the wallboard, taking care not to break the paper surface.

3. Interior trim and millwork: All exposed millwork shall be machine sanded to a smooth finish, with all joints tight and formed to conceal any shrinkage. Miter exterior angles, butt and cope interior angles, and scarf all running joints in moldings.

4. Hardwood flooring: All subfloors are to be broom cleaned and covered with deadening felt before the finished floor is laid. Wood flooring, where scheduled, is to be 1″ x 3″ T&G and end-matched select oak flooring. Flooring is to be laid evenly and blind nailed or stapled every 16″ without tool marks.

5. Closet rods: Furnish and install where indicated on drawings. Rods are to be adjustable chrome, fitted, and supported at least every 4′.

E. Cleanup

Upon completion of work, all surplus and waste materials shall be removed from the building, and the entire structure and involved portions of the site shall be left in a neat, clean, and acceptable condition.

FORMAT FOR SPECIFICATIONS

The format or style in which specifications are written varies depending on the nature of the project and the specification writer. The example shown in this unit is typical of specifications for a small project. Most specifications for large projects follow the format established by the Construction Specifications Institute *(CSI Format)*, figure 23-1, page 126. On very large projects there may be several hundred pages of specifications. Following the CSI Format makes the task of finding information easier.

On smaller projects a very brief form of specifications may be used. Figure 23-2, page 127, is a page of one style of brief specifications. Another common specification form is the Federal Housing Administration *Description of Materials*. This form is intended for construction to be financed by an F.H.A. loan, but is sometimes used for other projects.

DIVISION 1—GENERAL REQUIREMENTS

01010 SUMMARY OF WORK
01100 ALTERNATIVES
01150 MEASUREMENT & PAYMENT
01200 PROJECT MEETINGS
01300 SUBMITTALS
01400 QUALITY CONTROL
01500 TEMPORARY FACILITIES & CONTROLS
01600 MATERIAL & EQUIPMENT
01700 PROJECT CLOSEOUT

DIVISION 2—SITE WORK

02010 SUBSURFACE EXPLORATION
02100 CLEARING
02110 DEMOLITION
02200 EARTHWORK
02250 SOIL TREATMENT
02300 PILE FOUNDATIONS
02350 CAISSONS
02400 SHORING
02500 SITE DRAINAGE
02550 SITE UTILITIES
02600 PAVING & SURFACING
02700 SITE IMPROVEMENTS
02800 LANDSCAPING
02850 RAILROAD WORK
02900 MARINE WORK
02950 TUNNELING

DIVISION 3—CONCRETE

03100 CONCRETE FORMWORK
03150 FORMS
03200 CONCRETE REINFORCEMENT
03250 CONCRETE ACCESSORIES
03300 CAST-IN-PLACE CONCRETE
03350 SPECIALLY FINISHED (ARCHITECTURAL) CONCRETE
03360 SPECIALLY PLACED CONCRETE
03400 PRECAST CONCRETE
03500 CEMENTITIOUS DECKS
03600 GROUT

DIVISION 4—MASONRY

04100 MORTAR
04150 MASONRY ACCESSORIES
04200 UNIT MASONRY
04400 STONE
04500 MASONRY RESTORATION & CLEANING
04550 REFRACTORIES

DIVISION 5—METALS

05100 STRUCTURAL METAL FRAMING
05200 METAL JOISTS
05300 METAL DECKING
05400 LIGHTGAGE METAL FRAMING
05500 METAL FABRICATIONS
05700 ORNAMENTAL METAL
05800 EXPANSION CONTROL

DIVISION 6—WOOD & PLASTICS

06100 ROUGH CARPENTRY
06130 HEAVY TIMBER CONSTRUCTION
06150 TRESTLES
06170 PREFABRICATED STRUCTURAL WOOD
06200 FINISH CARPENTRY
06300 WOOD TREATMENT
06400 ARCHITECTURAL WOODWORK
06500 PREFABRICATED STRUCTURAL PLASTICS
06600 PLASTIC FABRICATIONS

DIVISION 7—THERMAL & MOISTURE PROTECTION

07100 WATERPROOFING
07150 DAMPPROOFING
07200 INSULATION
07300 SHINGLES & ROOFING TILES
07400 PREFORMED ROOFING & SIDING
07500 MEMBRANE ROOFING
07570 TRAFFIC TOPPING
07600 FLASHING & SHEET METAL
07800 ROOF ACCESSORIES
07900 SEALANTS

DIVISION 8—DOORS & WINDOWS

08100 METAL DOORS & FRAMES
08200 WOOD & PLASTIC DOORS
08300 SPECIAL DOORS
08400 ENTRANCES & STOREFRONTS
08500 METAL WINDOWS
08600 WOOD & PLASTIC WINDOWS
08650 SPECIAL WINDOWS
08700 HARDWARE & SPECIALTIES
08800 GLAZING
08900 WINDOW WALLS/CURTAIN WALLS

DIVISION 9—FINISHES

09100 LATH & PLASTER
09250 GYPSUM WALLBOARD
09300 TILE
09400 TERRAZZO
09500 ACOUSTICAL TREATMENT
09540 CEILING SUSPENSION SYSTEMS
09550 WOOD FLOORING
09650 RESILIENT FLOORING
09680 CARPETING
09700 SPECIAL FLOORING
09760 FLOOR TREATMENT
09800 SPECIAL COATINGS
09900 PAINTING
09950 WALL COVERING

DIVISION 10—SPECIALTIES

10100 CHALKBOARDS & TACKBOARDS
10150 COMPARTMENTS & CUBICLES
10200 LOUVERS & VENTS
10240 GRILLES & SCREENS
10260 WALL & CORNER GUARDS
10270 ACCESS FLOORING
10280 SPECIALTY MODULES
10290 PEST CONTROL
10300 FIREPLACES
10350 FLAGPOLES
10400 IDENTIFYING DEVICES
10450 PEDESTRIAN CONTROL DEVICES
10500 LOCKERS
10530 PROTECTIVE COVERS
10550 POSTAL SPECIALTIES
10600 PARTITIONS
10650 SCALES
10670 STORAGE SHELVING
10700 SUNCONTROLDEVICES(EXTERIOR)
10750 TELEPHONE ENCLOSURES
10800 TOILET & BATH ACCESSORIES
10900 WARDROBE SPECIALTIES

DIVISION 11—EQUIPMENT

11050 BUILT-IN MAINTENANCE EQUIPMENT
11100 BANK & VAULT EQUIPMENT
11150 COMMERCIAL EQUIPMENT
11170 CHECKROOM EQUIPMENT
11180 DARKROOM EQUIPMENT
11200 ECCLESIASTICAL EQUIPMENT
11300 EDUCATIONAL EQUIPMENT
11400 FOOD SERVICE EQUIPMENT
11480 VENDING EQUIPMENT
11500 ATHLETIC EQUIPMENT
11550 INDUSTRIAL EQUIPMENT
11600 LABORATORY EQUIPMENT
11630 LAUNDRY EQUIPMENT
11650 LIBRARY EQUIPMENT
11700 MEDICAL EQUIPMENT
11800 MORTUARY EQUIPMENT
11830 MUSICAL EQUIPMENT
11850 PARKING EQUIPMENT
11860 WASTE HANDLING EQUIPMENT
11870 LOADING DOCK EQUIPMENT
11880 DETENTION EQUIPMENT
11900 RESIDENTIAL EQUIPMENT
11970 THEATER & STAGE EQUIPMENT
11990 REGISTRATION EQUIPMENT

DIVISION 12—FURNISHINGS

12100 ARTWORK
12300 CABINETS & STORAGE
12500 WINDOW TREATMENT
12550 FABRICS
12600 FURNITURE
12670 RUGS & MATS
12700 SEATING
12800 FURNISHING ACCESSORIES

DIVISION 13—SPECIAL CONSTRUCTION

13010 AIR SUPPORTED STRUCTURES
13050 INTEGRATED ASSEMBLIES
13100 AUDIOMETRIC ROOM
13250 CLEAN ROOM
13350 HYPERBARIC ROOM
13400 INCINERATORS
13440 INSTRUMENTATION
13450 INSULATED ROOM
13500 INTEGRATED CEILING
13540 NUCLEAR REACTORS
13550 OBSERVATORY
13600 PREFABRICATED STRUCTURES
13700 SPECIAL PURPOSE ROOMS & BUILDINGS
13750 RADIATION PROTECTION
13770 SOUND & VIBRATION CONTROL
13800 VAULTS
13850 SWIMMING POOLS

DIVISION 14—CONVEYING SYSTEMS

14100 DUMBWAITERS
14200 ELEVATORS
14300 HOISTS & CRANES
14400 LIFTS
14500 MATERIAL HANDLING SYSTEMS
14570 TURNTABLES
14600 MOVING STAIRS & WALKS
14700 TUBE SYSTEMS
14800 POWERED SCAFFOLDING

DIVISION 15—MECHANICAL

15010 GENERAL PROVISIONS
15050 BASIC MATERIALS & METHODS
15180 INSULATION
15200 WATER SUPPLY & TREATMENT
15300 WASTE WATER DISPOSAL & TREATMENT
15400 PLUMBING
15500 FIRE PROTECTION
15600 POWER OR HEAT GENERATION
15650 REFRIGERATION
15700 LIQUID HEAT TRANSFER
15800 AIR DISTRIBUTION
15900 CONTROLS & INSTRUMENTATION

DIVISION 16—ELECTRICAL

16010 GENERAL PROVISIONS
16100 BASIC MATERIALS & METHODS
16200 POWER GENERATION
16300 POWER TRANSMISSION
16400 SERVICE & DISTRIBUTION
16500 LIGHTING
16600 SPECIAL SYSTEMS
16700 COMMUNICATIONS
16850 HEATING & COOLING
16900 CONTROLS & INSTRUMENTATION

Fig. 23-1 CSI format for specifications

SHEATHING

Outside walls shall be covered with . . . .
securely nailed. Roof sheathing shall be of. . . . .
. . . .
securely nailed to rafters.

SIDINGS

Siding, if any, to be . . . .

ROOFING

Shingles for roof to be . . . .
laid. . . . . .inches to weather using galvanized nails.

SIDEWALL SHINGLES

Sidewall shingles, if any, to be . . . .
. . . .

INSULATION AND PAPER

Sidewall insulation to be. . . . .
Top floor ceiling insulation to be . . . .
Building paper under shingles to be. . . . .
Building paper over sheathing to be. . . . .
Building paper between subfloor and finish floor to be . . . .

OUTSIDE FINISH

All lumber required for outside finish shall be. . . . .
. . . .

WINDOW AND DOOR FRAMES

All window and outside door frames as shown on plans shall be of sound clear pine, free from objectionable
defects. Outside casings . . . . .thick. Door sills shall be. . . . .
Assembled basement sash units, if any, shall be. . . . .
Assembled window units, if any, shall be . . . .
Assembled door units, if any, shall be . . . .

Fig. 23-2 Brief form of specifications

ASSIGNMENT

Questions

Refer to the specifications in the back of the textbook to answer the following questions.

1. What size lumber is used for the wood sills resting on the foundation?

   2"x6" Fir ✓

2. What material is used for the piers on the porch?

   Cut Bluestone ✓

3. How thick is the gravel fill under the basement floor?

   4" ✓

4. What grade or weight of aluminum is to be used for the aluminum flashing around the chimney?

   Aluminum 28 gage ✓

5. How is exterior trim to be finished?

   Stain (one coat) ✓

6. What is the material and thickness for the stair treads?

   Oak 5/4" ✓

7. What color is the kitchen floor?

   Color by Owner ✓

8. How much money is allowed for light fixtures?

   1,200.00 ✓

9. What company is specified as the manufacturer of the overhead fixed-sash windows?

   Wilson Millwork ✓

10. How thick is the insulation under the basement floor?

    2"

Glossary

Aggregate Hard materials, such as sand and crushed stone, that are used to make concrete

Anchor Bolt A bolt placed in the surface of concrete or masonry for attaching wood framing members

Apron A concrete slab at the approach to a garage door — also the wood trim below a window stool

Architect's Scale A flat or triangular scale used to measure scaled drawings

Ash Dump A small metal door in the bottom of a fireplace

Awning Window A window that is hinged near the top, so the bottom opens outward

Backfill Earth placed against a building wall after the foundation is in place

Backsplash The raised lip on the back edge of a countertop that prevents water from running down the backs of the cabinets

Balloon Framing A type of construction in which the studs are continuous from the sill to the top of the wall. The upper floor joists are supported by a let-in ribbon.

Balusters Vertical pieces which support a railing

Balustrade An assembly of balusters and a handrail

Batt Insulation Flexible, blanketlike pieces, usually of fiberglass, used for thermal or sound insulation

Batten Narrow strips of wood used to cover joints between boards of sheet metal

Batten Boards An arrangement of stakes and horizontal pieces used to attach lines for laying out a building

Beam Any major horizontal structural member

Board Foot One hundred-forty-four cubic inches of wood or the amount contained in a piece measuring $12'' \times 12'' \times 1''$

Bottom Chord The bottom horizontal member in a truss

Box Sill The header joist nailed across the ends of floor joists at the sill

Building Lines The outside edge of the exterior walls of a building

Casement Window A window that is hinged at one side so the opposite side opens outward

Casing The trim around a door or window

Centerline An actual or imaginary line through the exact center of any object

Chain Dimensions A series of dimensions for parts or features in a continuous line

Collar Beam Horizontal members that tie opposing rafters together, usually installed about halfway up the rafters

Column A metal post used to support an object above it

Common Rafter A rafter extending from the top of the wall to the ridge

Computer-Aided Drafting (CAD) The process of using computers to create drawings

Concrete Building material consisting of fine and coarse aggregates bonded together by portland cement

Contour Lines Lines on a topographic map or site plan that describe the contour of the land

Contract Any agreement in writing for one party to perform certain work and the other party to pay for the work

Convenience Outlet Electrical outlet provided for convenient use of lamps, appliances, and other electrical equipment

Cornice The construction which encloses the ends of the rafters at the top of the wall

Cornice Return The construction where the level cornice meets the sloping rake cornice

Course A single row of building units such as concrete blocks or shingles

Cove Mold Concave molding used to trim an inside corner

Damper A door installed in the throat of a fireplace to regulate the draft

Dampproofing The vapor barrier or coating on foundation walls or under concrete slabs that prevents moisture from entering the house

Datum A reference point from which elevations are measured

Detail A drawing showing special information about a particular part of the construction. The details are usually drawn to a larger scale than on other drawings and are sometimes section views.

Diazo Process A drawing reproduction process for making white prints

Double-hung Window A window consisting of two sash that slide up and down past one another

Drip Cap A wooden ledge over wall openings that prevents water from running back under the frame or trim around the opening

Drip Edge Metal trim installed at the edge of a roof to stop water from running back under the edge of the roof deck

Drywall Interior wall construction using gypsum wallboard

Elevation A drawing that shows vertical dimensions; it may also be the height of a point, usually in feet above sea level.

Fascia The part of a cornice that covers the ends of the rafters

Flashing Sheet metal used to cover openings and joints in walls and roofs

Floor Plan A drawing showing the arrangement of rooms, the locations of windows and doors, and the complete dimensions — it is actually a horizontal section through the entire building.

Flue The opening inside a chimney, usually formed by a terra cotta flue liner.

Flush door A door having flat surfaces

Footing The concrete base upon which the foundation walls are built

Footing Drain See Perimeter Drain.

Frieze A horizontal board beneath the cornice and against the wall above the siding

Frost Line The maximum depth to which frost penetrates the earth

Furring Narrow strips of wood attached to a surface for the purpose of creating a plumb or level surface for attaching the wall, ceiling, or floor surface

Gable The triangular area between the roof and the top plate of the walls at the ends of a gable roof

Gable Studs The studs placed between the end rafters and the top plates of the end walls

Gauge A standard unit of measurement for the diameter of wire or the thickness of sheet metal

Girder A beam that supports floor joists

Gypsum Wallboard Drywall materials made of gypsum encased in paper to form boards

Header A joist fastened across the ends of regular joists in an opening, or the framing member above a window or door opening

Hearth Concrete or masonry apron in front of a fireplace

Hip Outside corner formed by intersecting roofs

Hip Rafter The rafter extending from the corner of a building to the ridge at a hip

Insulated Glazing Two or more pieces of glass in a single sash with air space between them for the purpose of insulation

Isometric A kind of drawing in which horizontal lines are 30 degrees from true horizontal and vertical lines are vertical

Jack Rafter Rafter between the outside wall and a hip rafter or the ridge and a valley rafter

Jamb Side members of a door or window frame

Joists Horizontal framing members that support a floor or ceiling

Leader Line or arrow referencing information to a drawing

Lintel Steel or concrete member that spans a clear opening, usually found over doors, windows, and fireplace openings

Masonry Cement Cement that is especially prepared for making mortar

Mil A unit of measure for the thickness of very thin sheets — one mil equals 1.001″

Miter A 45-degree cut so that two pieces will form a 90-degree corner

Mortar A cement and aggregate mixture for bonding masonry units together

Mullion The vertical piece located between two windows that are installed side by side. Window units that include a mullion are called mullion windows.

Muntin Small vertical and horizontal strips that separate the individual panes of glass in a window sash

Nailer A piece of wood used in any of several places to provide a nailing surface for other framing members

Nominal Size The size by which a material is specified. The actual size is often slightly smaller.

Nosing The portion of a stair tread that projects beyond the riser

Orthographic Projection A method of drawing that shows separate views of an object

Panel Door A door made up of panels held in place by rails and stiles

Parging A thin coat of portland-cement plaster used to smooth masonry walls

Penny Size The length of nails

Perimeter Drain (also, Footing Drain) An underground drain pipe around the footings to carry ground water away from the building

Pilaster A masonry or concrete pier built as an integral part of a wall

Pitch Refers to the steepness of a roof — the pitch is written as a fraction with the rise over the span.

Plan Drawing of an object as viewed from above

Plate The horizontal framing members at the top and bottom of the wall studs

Platform Framing (also called Western Framing) A method of framing in which each level is framed separately. The subfloor is laid for each floor before the walls above it are formed.

Plumb Truly vertical or true according to a plumb bob

Portland Cement Finely powdered limestone material used to bond the aggregates together in concrete and mortar

R-value The ability of a material to resist the flow of heat

Rafter The framing members in a roof

Rail The horizontal members in a door, sash, or other panel construction

Rake The sloping cornice at the end of a gable roof

Ridge Board The framing member between the tops of rafters that runs the length of the ridge of a roof

Rise The vertical dimension of a roof or stair

Riser The vertical dimension of one step in a stair; the board enclosing the space between the two treads is called a riser.

Rough Opening The opening in framing or masonry used for a window or door.

Run The horizontal distance covered by an inclined surface such as a rafter or stair

Sash The frame holding the glass in a window

Saturated Felt Paperlike felt that has been treated with asphalt to make it water resistant

Screed A straight board used to level concrete immediately after it is placed

Section View A drawing showing what would be seen by cutting through a building or part

Setback The distance from a street or front property line to the front of a building

Sheathing The rough exterior covering over the framing members of a building

Shim Thin pieces, usually wood, used to build up low spots between framing and finish work

Sill The framing member in contact with a masonry or concrete foundation

Sill Sealer Compressible material used under the sill to seal any gaps

Site Plan The drawing that shows the boundaries of the building, its location, and site utilities

Sliding Window A window with two or more sash that slide horizontally past one another

Soffit The bottom surface of any part of a building, such as the underside of a cornice or lowered portion of a ceiling over wall cabinets

Span The horizontal dimension between vertical supports — the span of a beam is the distance between the posts that support it.

Specifications A written description of materials or construction

Square The amount of siding or roofing materials required to cover 100 square feet

Stair Carriage The supporting framework under a stair

Stile The vertical members in a sash, door, or other panel construction

Stool A trim piece that forms the finished window sill

Stop Molding that stops a door from swinging through the opening as it is closed. It is also used to hold the sash in place in a window frame

Stud Vertical framing members in a wall

Subfloor The first layer of rough flooring applied to the floor joists

Termite Shield A sheet-metal shield installed at the top of a foundation to prevent termites from entering the wood superstructure

Top Chord The top horizontal member of a truss

Tread The surface of a step in stair construction

Trimmers The double framing members at the sides of an opening

Truss A manufactured assembly used to support a load over a long span

Underlayment Any material installed over the subfloor to provide a smooth surface over which floor covering will be installed

Valley The inside corner formed by intersecting roofs

Valley Rafter The rafter extending from an inside corner in the walls to the ridge at a valley

Vapor Barrier Sheet material used to prevent water vapor from passing through a building surface

Veneer A thin covering — in masonry, a single wythe of finished masonry over a wall; in woodwork, a thin layer of thin wood

Vertical Contour Interval The difference in elevation between adjacent contour lines on a topographic map or site plan

Water Closet A plumbing fixture commonly called a toilet

Western Framing See Platform Framing.

Wythe A single thickness of masonry construction

INDEX

The foldouts attached to the inside back cover contain 6 drawings
and specifications.

1— Plot Plan
2— Foundation Plan
3— Floor Plan
4— Front Elevation and Rear Elevation
5— Right Elevation and Left Elevation
6— Details
7— Specifications